New Mexico

New Mexico

Deborah Kent

Children's Press®
A Division of Scholastic Inc.
New York   Toronto   London   Auckland   Sydney
Mexico City   New Delhi   Hong Kong
Danbury, Connecticut

Frontispiece: New Mexico is known for its remarkable beauty.

Front cover: Organ Mountains

Back cover: Inn at Santa Fe, Santa Fe

Consultant: Patricia Froehlich, New Mexico State Library

Please note: All statistics are as up-to-date as possible at the time of publication.

Book production by Editorial Directions, Inc.

Library of Congress Cataloging-in-Publication Data

Kent, Deborah.
    New Mexico / by Deborah Kent.
      144 p. 24 cm. — (America the beautiful. Second series)
    Includes bibliographical references and index.
      Summary : Describes the geography, plants, animals, history, economy, language,
    religions, culture, sports, arts, and people of New Mexico, where the three major
    cultures are Native American, Hispanic, and Anglo.
      ISBN 0-516-20690-7
      1. New Mexico—Juvenile literature. [1. New Mexico.] I. Title. II. Series.
    F796.3.K46   1999
    978.9—dc21   98-19576
                                                                                              CIP
                                                                                              A

Acknowledgments

The author wishes to express her special thanks to the staff members of the Santa Fe Visitors Bureau, the Albuquerque Museum, and the New Mexico Department of Tourism for their generous assistance during the writing of this book.

Bandelier National Monument

Pottery from Cliff Palace

New Mexican vista

Contents

Zia sun hot-air balloon

Zuni dancers

Santa Fe art gallery

Carlsbad Caverns

William Cody

CHAPTER ONE

Torching Old Man Gloom

At the Fiesta de Santa Fe, fireworks explode, and Zozobra, or Old Man Gloom, is set on fire.

"Isn't it time yet? How much longer?" Here and there in the crowded park children's voices rise with impatience. "Look at the sun," their parents answer. "Everything starts when the sun goes down."

The eager crowd stands in Fort Marcy Park in Santa Fe, New Mexico. On the Friday after Labor Day the park is the stage for the opening scenes of the city's biggest annual event, the Fiesta de Santa Fe. As the sun sinks, a band bursts into full swing. Dancers glide and spin to lively rhythms. But the children are still restless. Their eyes wander to a papier-mâché figure that towers high over their heads. Its long white robes shimmer in the darkness. The figure is known as Zozobra, or Old Man Gloom. It is said to represent the sadness and troubles of the preceding year.

At last comes the long-awaited moment. Fireworks crackle, lighting up the sky. Suddenly the head of Zozobra explodes into flame. The arms writhe as though in pain. Agonized groans rip the air. Tongues of fire race up and down the giant figure. Within minutes, nothing remains of Old Man Gloom but a twisted wire frame.

Visitors often think the burning of Zozobra is a Native American tradition. Actually, the first Zozobra figure was created in 1926 by Will Schuster, an artist of northern European, or Anglo, descent. Zozobra's arms move by remote control. An actor with a microphone produces his heart-stopping groans.

New Mexico today is home to three major cultures—Native

Opposite: A local man dressed as a conquistador at the Fiesta de Santa Fe

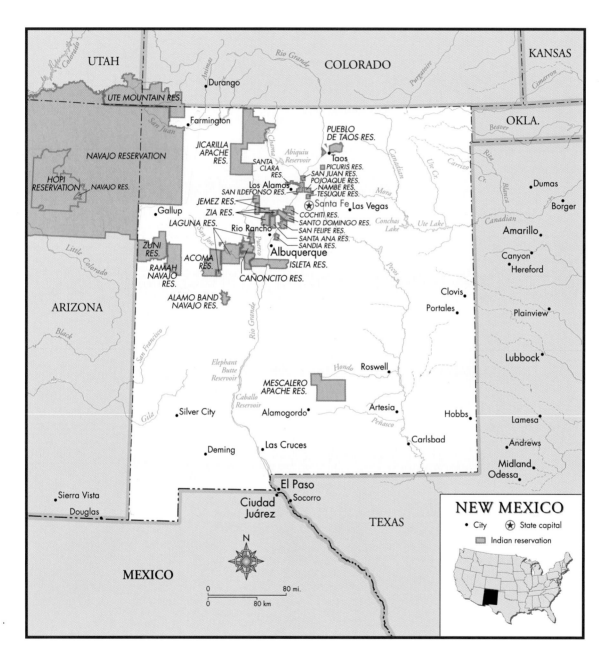

**Geopolitical map of
New Mexico**

Pottery and other
crafts for sale in
Santa Fe

American, Hispanic, and Anglo. Through a weekend of music, dancing, and delicious food, the Fiesta de Santa Fe reflects this rich cultural blend. American Indian women sell traditional pottery, woven baskets, and turquoise jewelry. Visitors munch Mexican tacos and tamales. Rock bands blare songs that are popular from New York to California.

Everywhere in New Mexico the three cultures survive and flourish. They braid together to form something that cannot be called Anglo or Hispanic or Native American, but only New Mexican. The New Mexicans are endlessly building their own unique traditions. Zozobra is one example. Each year at the Fiesta de Santa Fe, Zozobra erases the hard times of the year that has passed and makes way for a better year to come.

CHAPTER TWO

The Northern Frontier

Petroglyphs are reminders of ancient New Mexicans.

O n a September day in 1908, a cowboy named George McJunkin was mending fences near Folsom, New Mexico. A recent flash flood had carved a streambed into a deep gully. Peering over the rim, McJunkin saw that the gully was littered with enormous bones. Among them he found several stone spear points. For years, McJunkin tried to interest the world in his discovery. At last, in 1926, scientists recognized that the bones were those of a long-extinct bison species. Spear points embedded in some of the bones proved that human beings lived and hunted in present-day New Mexico more than 10,000 years ago.

Stone, Clay, and Corn

The stone spear points known today as Folsom points were about 3 inches (8 cm) in length. They were flat and leaf-shaped, with narrow grooves on either side. The people who made them hunted giant ground sloths, mammoths, and other large animals that are now extinct. They moved constantly, following the herds of animals that provided their food.

The early New Mexicans were the descendants of Asian peoples who reached North America more than 20,000 years ago. These ancient peoples crossed the Bering Strait from Siberia into Alaska. Gradually, people spread throughout North America. They

Opposite: Cliff dwellings at Bandelier National Monument

The Cowboy Scientist

George McJunkin (1851–1922) was born a slave on a ranch in Texas. As a free man after the Civil War, he worked on cattle ranches in northeastern New Mexico. Throughout his life, McJunkin was fascinated by the natural world. When he rode the range, he carried a small telescope so he could study the stars at night. McJunkin collected unusual specimens wherever he went—rocks, insects, lizards, and bones.

McJunkin spent the last fourteen years of his life trying to interest the scientific community in the spear points he had found near Folsom. He wrote to museums all over the country, inviting the experts to examine his finds. Sadly, no one saw the importance of McJunkin's discovery until after his death. When scientists finally did visit Folsom, they tried to claim the credit for this important discovery.

But the residents of Folsom never forgot the black cowboy with his telescope and his strange collections. In the 1960s, one old-timer told McJunkin's story to a newspaper reporter. At last, George McJunkin received the recognition he so long deserved. ■

came to New Mexico in several waves, or migrations. They found it to be a richly varied land. It offered fertile valleys and lush grasslands where game grazed in abundance. But there were also harsh, waterless deserts and rugged mountain ranges. It was not an easy land to tame.

In about A.D. 100, people known today as the Basket Makers settled in present-day New Mexico and Arizona. These people

Gifts from the South

One group of ancient people, known today as the Mogollon, moved to southwestern New Mexico from Mexico to the south. The Mogollon brought a valuable food plant called maize. Maize was the ancestor of today's corn. Later, Indians ground it into flour on a flat stone called a metate. The flour was mixed with water and patted into thin round cakes. These cakes, known as tortillas, are basic to Mexican and New Mexican cooking today.

The Mogollon also brought another valuable gift to New Mexico. They knew how to make pottery from the moist clay they found along rivers and streams. Pottery vessels gave people an easy way to carry food and water. Their use made it possible for people to live in inhospitable desert regions, where water had to be carried long distances. ■

wove beautiful, sturdy baskets from wild reeds. Some of these baskets were woven so tightly that they could hold water without leaking a drop. The Basket Makers lived in caves or in houses made of poles plastered with mud. Often they dug a pit in the ground for storing food.

As the centuries passed, the Basket Makers learned to plant corn and to make beautiful pottery. Their homes grew more and more elaborate. By about 1000, the descendants of the Basket Makers entered a spectacular era archaeologists call the Classic Pueblo Period. The people of this period are known today as the Anasazi. The name *Anasazi* comes from a Navajo Indian word meaning "ancestors."

The Anasazi of the Classic Pueblo Period are best known for their extraordinary achievements in architecture. Working with stone, plaster, and sun-dried bricks, they built complex structures with many connected rooms. Some of these dwellings clung to steep canyon walls. Others were perched on flat-topped hills called mesas. Like today's apartment buildings, the Anasazi complexes reached several stories in height. The stories rose in a series of

Some Anasazi lived in homes that clung to canyon walls.

steps. The roofs of one story formed porches for the story above. The Anasazi climbed to their homes by means of strong wooden ladders. If enemies threatened, the Anasazi pulled the ladders up into their homes for safety.

Sometime around A.D. 1300 the Anasazi abandoned their canyon strongholds. No one knows for sure why their civilization suddenly crumbled. Perhaps they were under attack from powerful enemies. They may have been stricken with an epidemic. The most likely explanation seems to be that the region suffered a severe drought for several years. By studying the growth rings of ancient trees, scientists know that rainfall became very scarce between the years 1276 and 1299.

The Master Builders

The most spectacular Anasazi complex that survives today is Cliff Palace at Chaco Canyon in New Mexico's northwestern corner. The Cliff Palace complex had nearly one thousand rooms and probably housed several hundred families. Many of the rooms have large pits called kivas. The kivas were used in religious ceremonies.

The Anasazi made richly painted pottery with intricate animal and geometric designs. They raised turkeys and kept dogs as companions. They planted corn, squash, beans, and melons. Both men and women wore beads of turquoise, quartz, and seashells. Their use of shells indicates that they traded with other peoples who lived near the sea. ■

The Anasazi scattered to the east and south. They resettled in small villages known today as pueblos, from the Spanish word meaning "towns." The people themselves are generally called the Pueblo as well. By the early 1500s, many distinct Pueblo groups lived in New Mexico. These included the Hopi, Zuni, Tewa, Acoma, and Jemez. Each spoke its own language and had its own customs and ceremonies. The Pueblo continued to farm and to make their handsome pottery. But they never again built magnificent cliffside palaces.

At about the time the Anasazi left Chaco Canyon, a fresh wave of migrants entered New Mexico. They were nomadic, or wandering, hunters skilled with the bow and arrow. They seldom stayed in one place long enough to plant crops or build permanent homes. Today we refer to these people as the Navajo and the Apache. For more than two centuries the Pueblo, Apache, and Navajo fought and made peace, struggling for food and other resources. Then, early in the 1500s, came warnings of yet another migration, one that would change the region forever.

Hernando Cortés was a Spanish soldier who conquered the Aztec empire in Mexico.

The Sword and the Cross

In 1521, a Spanish soldier named Hernando Cortés conquered Mexico's Aztec empire. After destroying the Aztec capital city, the Spaniards founded a mighty empire of their own. They extended their power across Mexico and into Central and South America. Their empire was referred to as New Spain.

Nothing thrilled the Spaniards more than the thought of gold. From their capital in Mexico City, they sent gold-seeking expeditions in every direction. Fleets of treasure ships carried splendid cargoes back to Spain.

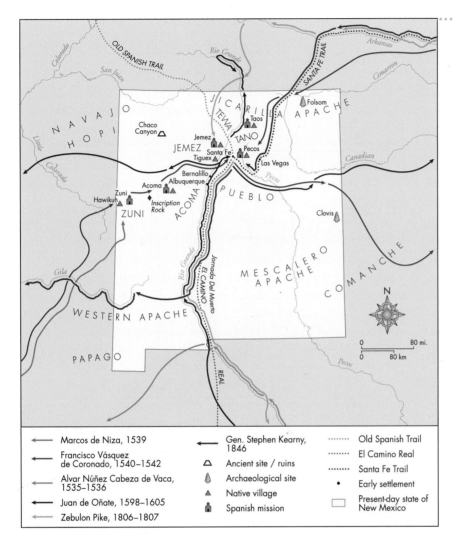

Exploration of New Mexico

Legend		
Marcos de Niza, 1539	Gen. Stephen Kearny, 1846	Old Spanish Trail
Francisco Vásquez de Coronado, 1540–1542	Ancient site / ruins	El Camino Real
Alvar Núñez Cabeza de Vaca, 1535–1536	Archaeological site	Santa Fe Trail
Juan de Oñate, 1598–1605	Native village	Early settlement
Zebulon Pike, 1806–1807	Spanish mission	Present-day state of New Mexico

Yet the Spaniards hungered for more. They were so obsessed with gold that the Native Americans believed they suffered from a strange form of madness.

In addition to searching for gold, the Spaniards had a second purpose in the Americas. They believed it was their mission to save the souls of the Native Americans. Hundreds of priests worked to convert the native peoples to Roman Catholicism. Often the Indians were baptized at the point of a sword.

All That Glisters Is Not Gold

One day, four bedraggled men stumbled into a Spanish settlement in Mexico. Years before, they had been shipwrecked on the coast of Florida. Somehow they made their way across present-day Texas and New Mexico until they reached Spanish Mexico. The men claimed they had seen seven fabulous cities, the Seven Cities of Cibola. They said the people of these cities wore so much gold and silver that they bowed beneath its weight. Their houses were encrusted with gold.

In 1539, a Spanish friar, or traveling priest, led a small exploring party into the country north of Mexico. His name was Father Marcos de Niza. Marcos de Niza hoped to find the fantastic seven cities. His guide was one of the shipwreck survivors, an African slave named Esteban. On the journey northward, Esteban hurried ahead as a scout. If he found gold, he promised to send a messenger back to Marcos de Niza with a wooden cross. The bigger the cross, the greater the treasure he had discovered.

Eagerly the friar waited for news. At last, a messenger staggered into camp, carrying a heavy wooden cross nearly six feet tall. Marcos de Niza rushed to catch up with Esteban, sure that a store of riches awaited him. From a hilltop he saw Hawikuh, a town whose houses sparkled in the sun. This must be one of the famous Seven Cities! But the people of Hawikuh had killed Esteban. Marcos de Niza was afraid to draw closer. He planted a cross on the hilltop and claimed the entire region for the king of Spain. Then he hastened back to Mexico with his story.

The following year, a major expedition set out from Mexico under Francisco Vásquez de Coronado. Marcos de Niza served as Coronado's guide. Retracing his earlier journey, Marcos led Coronado to Hawikuh. The inhabitants quickly surrendered, overwhelmed by the thundering horses and flashing swords of the soldiers. To the Spaniards' dismay, the village was only a collection of huts made of whitewashed bricks. From a distance, their huts sparkled like gold. But not an ounce of the precious metal was to be found. ■

Charting a New Land

Francisco Vásquez de Coronado (1510–1554) was among the first Europeans to explore and map much of the U.S. Southwest. Coronado set up a base camp near present-day Bernalillo, New Mexico. From there, he and his men fanned out to the north, east, and west. In their search for gold, they crossed burning deserts and barren lava flows. They trekked over the tall-grass plains of eastern New Mexico into Texas. Pushing northward, they braved deserts and scaled mountains.

Finally, in 1542, Coronado returned to Mexico City. He had claimed a vast swath of new territory for the Spanish Crown. But he was a deeply disappointed man. Despite all the hardships he endured, he reached Mexico City empty-handed. He had never found gold. ▨

From time to time over the next fifty years, Spanish priests ventured into the territory north of Mexico. They did their best to convert the people they found, but they were usually driven away. Then, in 1598, a rich mine owner named Juan de Oñate led some 400 Spanish settlers to the western bank of the Rio Grande. There he established San Juan de los Caballeros, later renamed San Gabriel. San Gabriel was the first capital of the region the Spaniards called Nuevo Mexico, or New Mexico.

In 1610, the governor of New Spain sent Pedro de Peralta to establish a new capital farther up the Rio Grande. Peralta gave his settlement the unwieldy name of La Villa Real de la Santa Fe de San Francisco de Asis (Royal City of the Holy Faith of St. Francis of Assisi). The capital was known simply as Santa Fe.

There was no gold in New Mexico, but there were thousands of souls to be saved among the Pueblo. Catholic missionary priests

The Oldest Capital

People tend to think of Boston, Massachusetts, as the oldest state capital in the United States. Boston was established in 1630. It was the first capital in the thirteen English colonies on the Atlantic Coast. But Santa Fe, the capital of New Mexico in New Spain, was founded twenty years earlier, in 1610. Santa Fe is the oldest capital city in the nation. ■

plunged wholeheartedly into the task. They baptized the Pueblo in village after village, usually by threatening them with death. Once the Pueblo became Christians, the priests treated them as slaves. They forbade them to practice any of their ancient ceremonies. The Pueblo were forced to build a splendid palace for the governor in Santa Fe. Their labor built mission churches all over New Mexico.

This mission church in Laguna was built in 1642.

Despite Spanish laws, many of the Pueblo practiced their tribal religions in secret. In 1680, a Pueblo medicine man named Popé led his people to revolt. The Pueblo attacked Santa Fe and killed about 400 Spaniards. The survivors abandoned the city and fled south. Triumphant, the Pueblo tore down the hated churches. Only the Governor's Palace remained as a reminder of Spanish rule.

A Leader of His People

As a young man, Popé (?–1688) learned the religious ceremonies of the Tewa Pueblo. All such rituals were forbidden by the Spaniards and had to be practiced in secret. Popé was deeply distressed by the cruelty of the Spaniards toward the Pueblo people. After he led a successful revolt in 1680, he tried to destroy every trace of the hated Spanish rule.

After the Spaniards fled from New Mexico, Popé became chief over several Pueblo villages. Unfortunately, he was sometimes as cruel as the Spaniards had been. In 1688, the Pueblo rebelled against Popé, and he was overthrown by his own people. ■

The Conquering Lady

When the Spanish colonists fled from Santa Fe in 1680, they carried a small wooden statue of the Virgin Mary. During their exile, the refugees prayed to the Virgin for help. When de Vargas reconquered Santa Fe in 1692, the Spaniards believed she had answered their prayers. Forever afterward, they treated the statue with special reverence. It was called Our Lady of the Rosary, the Conqueror. The original statue still stands in a chapel of Santa Fe's St. Francis Cathedral. Today, "the Conqueror" has been renamed "the Unifier." The little figure of the Virgin Mary is hailed as a bringer of peace. ■

The Royal Road

The Pueblo held Santa Fe for only twelve years. In 1692, the newly appointed governor of New Mexico, Diego de Vargas, led 300 soldiers from El Paso in present-day Texas. De Vargas reached Santa Fe on September 13. The Pueblo were outnumbered and surrendered without a fight. The next day de Vargas raised the Spanish flag over the Governor's Palace. New Mexicans celebrate de Vargas's reconquest each September with the Fiesta de Santa Fe.

Year by year, New Spain sent more friars and settlers to New Mexico. They restored ruined churches and established new missions. To keep the peace, the friars let the Indians practice some of their non-Christian traditions.

In our age of jet travel and E-mail, it is hard for us to conceive how isolated the New Mexicans were. A grinding six-month journey separated Santa Fe from Mexico City. One exchange of letters could take a year or more. When they moved to New Mexico, families cut their ties with everyone they knew.

Written in Stone

Near Zuni Pueblo in western New Mexico stands a sandstone cliff covered with messages. Some are petroglyphs —picture writing carved by the American Indians long before the arrival of the Spaniards. Other messages are written in Spanish and English. The cliff is known as Inscription Rock.

One of the most famous messages on Inscription Rock was carved by Juan de Oñate on his return from an expedition to the Gulf of California. Translated from Spanish, it reads: PASSED BY HERE THE GOVERNOR DON JUAN DE OÑATE FROM THE DISCOVERY OF THE SEA OF THE SOUTH, THE 16TH OF APRIL, 1605. Pedro de Vargas left another inscription: HERE WAS THE GENERAL DON PEDRO DE VARGAS, WHO CONQUERED FOR OUR HOLY FAITH AND FOR THE ROYAL CROWN ALL OF NEW MEXICO AT HIS OWN EXPENSE IN THE YEAR OF OUR LORD 1692.

Inscription Rock is preserved as part of El Morro National Monument. Today, a chain-link fence deters visitors who might be tempted to add new inscriptions of their own. ■

The Duke's Namesake

In 1706, New Mexico's governor, Francisco Cuervo y Valdes, decided to expand Spanish settlement on the Rio Grande. He moved thirty families from Bernalillo to a site south of Santa Fe. The governor named the settlement for the Duke of Albuquerque, a Spanish noble. Albuquerque's first houses clustered around its central square (above), or plaza. The settlement grew as ranches spread.

For years, Albuquerque, New Mexico, was nothing but a sleepy outpost on the river. It was far overshadowed by the capital to the north. In the eighteenth century, no one could have guessed that one day Albuquerque would be the most important city in New Mexico. ■

The only link between New Mexico and New Spain was El Camino Real, the Royal Road. Settlers and traders traveled this trail in lumbering caravans. They piled their boxes and bundles onto two-wheeled oxcarts called *carretas*. They also brought along herds of sheep, cattle, and pigs, and cages full of squawking chickens.

The worst portion of the Camino Real was known as the Jornada del Muerto, or Journey of the Dead. It was a three-day stretch through the desert country north of present-day Las Cruces. The sun beat down mercilessly during the day, but at night the temperature plunged below freezing. At any moment, caravans might be attacked by a band of Navajo or Apache warriors. The Native Americans resented the Spaniards for invading their traditional lands.

New Mexico was a remote, sparsely settled province on New Spain's northern frontier. For two centuries, it was largely left to manage its own affairs. New Spain had more pressing concerns.

By the dawn of the nineteenth century, Spain had been weakened by a series of European wars. Its vast empire began to crumble. In 1821, Mexico broke away from the mother country and became an independent republic.

The New Mexicans greeted the news with church bells, cannonades, and dancing in the streets. In Santa Fe, the last of the Spanish governors packed his belongings and departed forever. A governor from Mexico arrived to take his place. A new era was about to begin.

Into the Wider World

The Taos Valley

When Zebulon Pike entered New Mexico in 1806, he did not get a warm welcome. Pike was exploring western territory for the U.S. Army. Spanish soldiers promptly arrested him as a spy. They questioned him in Santa Fe and seized his notes and maps. He was escorted out of Spanish territory, never to return.

Despite his chilly reception, Pike was impressed by New Mexico. He wrote a glowing account of its grassy plains, stunning mountains, and fertile valleys. Pike's description sparked American interest in New Mexico and opened the way for a new migration.

Stars and Stripes Forever!

In 1806, the United States was a young and growing nation. Three years earlier, it had doubled its territory when it had bought a vast tract of land from France called the Louisiana Purchase. Now Americans were looking hungrily at land in the Southwest.

New Spain had discouraged contact between New Mexico and

Opposite: Traveling by wagon train on the Santa Fe Trail

Explorer or Spy?

Zebulon Pike (1779–1813) was born in New Jersey and joined the U.S. Army at the age of fifteen. He remained a professional soldier for the rest of his life. In 1805, General James Wilkinson ordered Pike to lead an exploring expedition into the northern region of New Spain, now the U.S. Southwest. Pike explored the Red and Arkansas Rivers. In present-day Colorado, he sighted Pikes Peak, the famous mountain that still bears his name.

Pike's explorations ended abruptly when he was captured by Spanish troops in northern New Mexico and accused of being a spy.

Today, some historians suspect that Pike may indeed have been spying on the Spaniards. General Wilkinson, who sent him on his expedition, was plotting an assault against New Spain. Aaron Burr, a former vice president of the United States, was apparently involved in the scheme. Pike's information may have aided Wilkinson and Burr.

Zebulon Pike went on to serve in the War of 1812, fought between the United States and Great Britain. He died in an unsuccessful raid on the Canadian city of York. ■

the United States to the east. But the Republic of Mexico took a broader view. In 1822, a year after Mexico gained independence, an American trader named William Becknell (1796?–1865) crossed the plains from Missouri. He rumbled into Santa Fe with a caravan loaded with goods. Becknell had calico cloth, knives, axes, kettles, mirrors, clocks, and a host of other surprises. The New Mexicans bought up everything he had to offer. Eagerly they traded leather, furs, and Mexican silver for goods from U.S. factories. Becknell's route from Independence, Missouri, to Santa Fe is remembered as the Santa Fe Trail.

The Lure of the Trail

For almost sixty years, the Santa Fe Trail served as the major highway between the Southwest and the eastern cities of the United States. For much of its length the trail followed the Missouri and Arkansas Rivers. Three branches all led into Santa Fe. The shortest and most often used branch was called the Cimarron Cutoff.

The Santa Fe Trail awakened U.S. interest in the rich resources of New Spain's northern territory. As the years passed, the trail brought a stream of U.S. settlers into the Southwest.

Despite the many hardships suffered by travelers, the Santa Fe Trail became a western legend. In some places the ruts left by thousands of wagon wheels can still be seen. ▪

Year by year, English-speaking people from the United States poured into Spanish-speaking New Mexico. Many were traders who came and went. Others saw New Mexico as a land of possibilities. Like the Spaniards before them, they planted crops, herded sheep and cattle, and searched for precious minerals.

In 1836, U.S. settlers in Texas, New Mexico's neighbor to the east, broke away from Mexico. Texas formed a nation of its own, the Lone Star Republic. After ten years of independence, the

Stephen W. Kearny's troops leaving Las Vegas, New Mexico, in August 1846

Texans decided to join the United States. Mexico was outraged. Most Mexicans felt that Texas still belonged to them. The conflict over Texas led the United States and Mexico into war.

The United States was fighting for more than Texas. Many U.S. citizens thought it was God's will that their nation should stretch from the Atlantic to the Pacific Ocean. This idea is referred to as manifest destiny. Believers in manifest destiny wanted Texas, California, and all of the Mexican land in between, including New Mexico.

On August 15, 1846, General Stephen W. Kearny (1794–1848) marched into the town of Las Vegas, New Mexico. To a crowd on the town square, he announced that New Mexico was now part of the United States. The U.S. troops met no resistance and marched on to Santa Fe. There Kearny declared himself the new territorial governor. Leaving Charles Bent (1799–1847), his deputy governor, in charge, Kearny moved on to California.

Trouble in Taos

The conquest of New Mexico was not wholly free from bloodshed. After the U.S. takeover, small rebellions broke out here and there throughout the territory. In January 1847, Charles Bent, governor of New Mexico, was murdered during a revolt in the town of Taos. U.S. forces surrounded Taos Pueblo and fired on rebels who took refuge in the church. The rebels finally surrendered. ■

The Mexican-American War was over in 1848. The treaty ceded a huge expanse of territory to the United States. It included New Mexico, Arizona, and parts of California, Nevada, Utah, and Colorado. Above the Palace of the Governors in Santa Fe floated the Stars and Stripes.

The Anglo Invasion

In 1850, Congress officially made New Mexico a U.S. territory. Bands of settlers rushed into the newly opened land. Most were cattle ranchers from Texas looking for fresh grasslands. The Spanish New Mexicans referred to the newcomers as Anglos.

Historical map of New Mexico

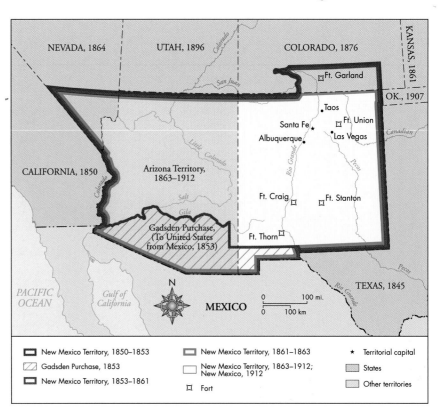

NEVADA, 1864   UTAH, 1896   COLORADO, 1876   KANSAS, 1861

Ft. Garland

OK., 1907

Taos
Santa Fe ★   Ft. Union
Albuquerque   Las Vegas

CALIFORNIA, 1850

Arizona Territory, 1863–1912

Ft. Craig   Ft. Stanton

Gadsden Purchase, (To United States from Mexico, 1853)

Ft. Thorn

PACIFIC OCEAN   Gulf of California   N   MEXICO   TEXAS, 1845

0   100 mi.
0   100 km

New Mexico Territory, 1850–1853   New Mexico Territory, 1861–1863   ★ Territorial capital

Gadsden Purchase, 1853   New Mexico Territory, 1863–1912; New Mexico, 1912   States

New Mexico Territory, 1853–1861   ⛿ Fort   Other territories

Drawing the Lines

Originally, New Mexico Territory extended south only to the Gila River. But it reached far to the west, including all of present-day Arizona. With the Gadsden Purchase of 1853, the federal government bought a new tract of land from Mexico. Much of this new land was added to New Mexico, expanding the territory southward into the "boot-heel" section. In 1863, Congress divided New Mexico Territory in two, creating the territory of Arizona. At last, New Mexico achieved the boundaries it still has today. ▩

New Mexico became a U.S. territory in a time of turmoil. The nation was torn over the issue of slavery. Hispanic New Mexicans took little interest in the debate. They often treated the Pueblo as if they were slaves. But they had no tradition of enslaving African-Americans. New Mexico's Anglos, however, took a proslavery stance. Most of them had grown up with slavery in the southern United States.

Tensions between the Northern and Southern states erupted into civil war in 1861. The South broke away from the Union to form the Confederate States of America. Confederate leaders hoped to extend their territory to California. As a first step, General H. H. Sibley led 2,300 Confederate troops across the Texas border into New Mexico. On February 21, 1862, Sibley defeated Union forces at Valverde. The Confederates swept onward, seizing Albuquerque and Santa Fe. A force of Union volunteers from Colorado came to the rescue. The Colorado troops ambushed the Confederates at Glorieta Pass, 15 miles (24 km) southeast of Santa Fe. After a fierce battle, the Confederates were on the run. They retreated across the territory, driven back in one skirmish after another. By August 1862, the Civil War in New Mexico was over.

Glorieta Pass was the spot where Union forces from Colorado defeated General Sibley's Confederate troops during the Civil War.

As more and more Anglos pushed into New Mexico, the Navajo and Apache watched their hunting grounds turn into farmland. Their nomadic way of life was deeply threatened. Hoping to drive out the intruders, the Native Americans attacked settlements throughout the territory. They burned homes, stole livestock, and killed whole families.

The U.S. Army sent General James Carleton (1814–1873) to "subdue" the native peoples. Carleton showed them no mercy. He ordered his soldiers to take all Navajo and Apache women and children prisoner. They were to kill native men on sight, whenever and wherever they were found. To carry out his campaign, Carleton appointed Colonel Christopher "Kit" Carson.

Carson had lived among the American Indians for many years. He spoke several Native American languages and knew the customs of many tribes. Yet he carried out Carleton's orders without question. In southern New Mexico, he attacked the Apache group known as the Mescalero. After three months of brutal fighting, the

Kit Carson, Mountain Man

When he was fifteen, Kit Carson (1809–1868) ran away from his home in Missouri. He joined a caravan of traders heading west on the Santa Fe Trail. Until 1842, Carson lived by trapping beavers and trading for furs with the American Indians of the Southwest. Along with serving in the Army and leading several military campaigns against Native Americans, he served as a guide on many exploring and military expeditions because he knew the country so well.

Kit Carson never learned to read or write. But he wanted to pass the story of his adventurous life to future generations. Carson dictated his autobiography to a friend in 1856.

In 1868, Carson was appointed superintendent of Indian affairs for the Colorado Territory. He held this position until his death. ■

Thousands of Navajo were captured by Kit Carson and imprisoned at Bosque Redondo.

Apache surrendered. Carson herded the survivors onto the Bosque Redondo Reservation on the Pecos River.

Next Carson turned his attention to the Navajo. Unlike the Apache, the Navajo depended on corn and sheep as well as hunting. Carson destroyed their crops and slaughtered their animals. On the edge of starvation, the Navajo finally submitted. Carson disobeyed one of Carleton's orders, sparing the lives of the Navajo men. But he herded the entire tribe—some 7,000 people—to Bosque Redondo. Food supplies were pitifully low on the 300-mile (480-km) journey. The Navajo had few blankets to shield them from winter storms. Hundreds died along the way. To this day, the Navajo date events as happening before or after the "Long Walk" of 1864.

The situation was even worse when the Navajo reached the reservation. The land was too dry for raising crops. Families were ravaged by hunger and disease. The Mescalero fled the reservation in 1866. Two years later, the federal government admitted that Bosque Redondo was a disaster. The government let the Navajo return to their traditional territory in northwestern New Mexico and eastern Arizona. The Navajo Nation still lives on this land today.

Wild and Woolly

New Mexico Territory was a lawless land during the 1870s and 1880s. Rootless men poured in, hoping to get rich quickly on newly discovered gold and silver. Few made their fortunes. But they found plenty of people eager to take what money they had. Mining towns such as Grants and Elizabethtown were raucous with saloons, cheap hotels, and gambling houses.

On the eastern plains, cattlemen grazed huge herds of steers. Cattle rustling, or stealing, was widespread. Ranchers often took the law into their own hands, shooting suspected rustlers on sight.

Through the 1870s, wagon trains continued to make their way along the rutted Santa Fe Trail. Then, in 1878, work crews completed the Atchison, Topeka, and Santa Fe Railroad. In 1881, the final stretch of the Southern Pacific Railroad was opened. Railroad lines made the old Santa Fe Trail obsolete. They brought New Mexicans closer than ever before to eastern markets. Mail traveled faster. Friends and family could visit more often. New Mexicans truly began to feel that they were part of the United States.

In the late 1800s, railroads were built in New Mexico.

Defense in Time of War

In 1851, the U.S. Army built Fort Union near the town of Watrous, New Mexico. For the rest of the nineteenth century, Fort Union was the biggest military installation in the U.S. Southwest. Fort Union was designated a national monument in 1954. Today, visitors can view the old fort's crumbling walls, brick chimneys, and officers' quarters. Push a button and a bugle call rings out as it must have sounded more than a hundred years ago. ▪

With the coming of the railroad, New Mexicans started pushing for statehood. Many people in Congress were reluctant to see the territory join the Union. New Mexico had a very high proportion of Hispanic and Native American residents. Their languages and customs were different from those of people back East. Some members of Congress questioned whether these people

The Kid from Silver City

In 1878, two businessmen, Alexander McSween and John Tunstall, opened a store in the town of Lincoln, New Mexico. Lawrence Murphy, a rival shopkeeper, was furious. When Tunstall was shot and killed, his friends thought Murphy was to blame. Everyone in Lincoln County took sides. For years, fighting raged between Murphy's supporters and supporters of McSween. The conflict is remembered as the Lincoln County War.

One of McSween's men was a cold-blooded killer who always wore a boyish grin. He was known as Billy the Kid. Billy the Kid was born William Henry McCarty (1859–1880) in Brooklyn, New York. When he was thirteen, he moved with his mother to Silver City, New Mexico. At seventeen, Billy the Kid shot a man who insulted him. The deed plunged him into a life of crime. In 1880, he claimed he had killed twenty-one men, one for each year of his life. Billy the Kid was finally killed by Sheriff Pat Garrett, who described the fatal encounter in his autobiography. The Kid's violent life has inspired novels, movies, and even a ballet. ■

could ever be "true Americans." Could people from such a different background be loyal U.S. citizens?

In 1911, New Mexico called a convention to draw up a state constitution. By act of Congress on January 6, 1912, New Mexico became the nation's forty-seventh state.

CHAPTER FOUR

Adobe and Atoms

Ernest Blumenschein next to his wagon with a broken wheel. This accident led him and Bert Phillips into Taos for the first time.

The prairie around Roswell, New Mexico, was quiet and empty in 1930. For physicist Robert Goddard, it was the ideal location. Goddard hoped to create models of liquid-fueled rockets that some day could carry humans into outer space. In New Mexico his noisy experiments disturbed no one but the ravens. Today, Goddard is called the Father of Rocket Science.

Like Goddard, thousands of other scientists have made the prairies and deserts of New Mexico their laboratory. Scientists are among the many groups of newcomers drawn to New Mexico in the twentieth century. Since the late nineteenth century, artists, writers, those people with lung ailments, among others, have sought out life in New Mexico for its climate, air, and landscape.

The Lure of Open Spaces

When his buggy broke a wheel on a rocky New Mexico road, Ernest Blumenschein was annoyed by the delay. He and his friend Bert Phillips headed to the nearby town of Taos for repairs. Blumenschein and Phillips were both painters. As they approached Taos, they were dazzled by the play of light across the landscape. "No artist had ever recorded the New Mexico I was now seeing,"

Opposite: A liftoff at the White Sands Missile Range

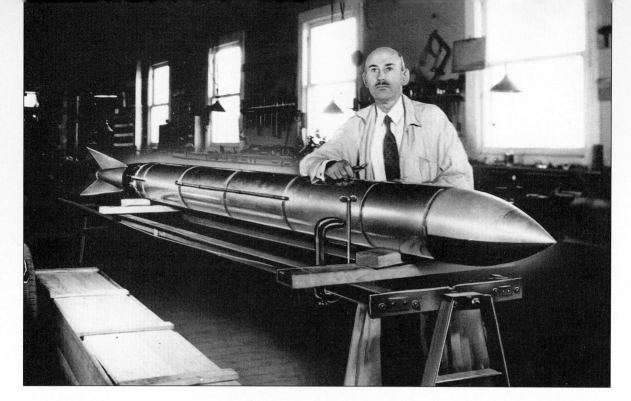

Breaking with Gravity

For most of his life, Robert Hutchings Goddard (1882–1945) was fascinated by rockets. Goddard was born in Massachusetts and earned a Ph.D. in physics at Clark University. In 1926, he published an article suggesting that someday human beings would be able to reach the moon. The article aroused much criticism and ridicule.

During the 1930s, Goddard worked at a laboratory near Roswell, New Mexico. He tackled the major problem in rocketry—the need for a liftoff powerful enough to break the force of gravity.

After his death, Goddard was awarded the Congressional Gold Medal. The National Aeronautics and Space Administration (NASA) named the Goddard Institute for Space Study at New York's Columbia University in honor of his contributions. ■

Blumenschein wrote later. "I was receiving the first great unforgettable inspiration of my life. My destiny was being decided."

Blumenschein and Phillips discovered the beauty of Taos in 1898. Their enthusiasm attracted more artists from back East. Painters, photographers, sculptors, and writers were thrilled by New Mexico's red sandstone cliffs and purple sunsets. They were captivated by the Spanish and Native American cultures that flour-

Picturing Taos

As a young man, Ernest Blumenschein (1874–1960) studied painting at the Academie Julian in Paris. He sometimes grew bored painting bowls of fruit as his teachers instructed him. Even doing portraits began to make him restless. In 1898, a painter friend, Joseph Henry Sharp, urged Blumenschein to visit the U.S. Southwest.

Blumenschein first saw Taos in 1898. In the decades that followed, he returned as often as he could. He worked in New York and Chicago during the winters, earning enough money to spend his summers in New Mexico. Blumenschein helped Taos develop as a colony for artists. He encouraged painters, sculptors, writers, and photographers to seek inspiration in the deserts and mountains.

Many of Blumenschein's paintings are abstract, brightly colored forms that remind one of the designs on Pueblo pottery. He could also paint in realistic detail. Some of his best-known works are portraits of Native Americans from Taos Pueblo. Blumenschein's *Ourselves and Taos Friends* shows a group of people gathered in an adobe house. ■

The beauty of Taos brought many people to the region.

ished in the towns and pueblos. As the years passed, Taos emerged as a thriving artist colony. Painters and writers made their homes in many other parts of the state as well.

In the 1890s and early 1900s, another group of people streamed into New Mexico. They were people with tuberculosis, or TB—a chronic disease of the lungs. In those days, there were no antibiotics to treat TB. Doctors believed that clean mountain air had healing powers and often prescribed a trip west for their patients.

Many of the TB patients who headed west were desperately ill. New Mexico was their last hope. Some died on the long, rough journey by train or stagecoach. But those who reached New Mexico played an important part in the state's development. New Mexicans referred to the newcomers as "lungers." Long-term hospitals called sanatoriums became a major business in New Mexico. Seventeen sanatoriums opened in

Chasing Pancho Villa

Francisco "Pancho" Villa (1878–1923) was the son of a poor farm laborer in northern Mexico. In his early teens, Villa killed a wealthy landowner who had assaulted his sister. Villa fled into the mountains, where he lived by his wits as a fugitive from the authorities.

When revolution broke out in Mexico in 1910, Villa fought against the dictator Porfirio Díaz. He proved to be a fearless soldier. He had a remarkable ability to recruit fighters from Mexico's poor. But Villa quarreled with other leaders and struggled endlessly for power.

Pancho Villa's 1916 raid on Columbus, New Mexico, marked only the second time that the United States was invaded by a foreign power. (The first was the British attack on Washington, D.C., in 1814, during the War of 1812.) U.S. citizens were outraged by Villa's brazen attack. President Woodrow Wilson sent General John Pershing in pursuit of Villa with 6,000 troops, but Villa was never caught. He became governor of the Mexican state of Chihuahua and was assassinated in 1923. ■

Albuquerque alone. Patients who recovered often stayed on, making New Mexico their permanent home. Many were educated people who worked to enhance the state's schools, libraries, and museums.

Surrounded by natural beauty, it was easy for New Mexicans to forget the world outside. But sometimes their peace was shattered by events beyond the state's boundaries. In 1910, a bloody revolution broke out in Mexico to the south. Poor peasants fought for the chance to own their own land. In March 1916, the Mexican general Pancho Villa swept across the border into the town of Columbus.

The townspeople woke to thudding hoofbeats, shouts, and the roar of gunfire. Villa's men rushed through the streets, shooting and looting. When they disappeared back across the border, sixteen New Mexicans lay dead.

In the 1920s, the United States began to change rapidly as automobiles became popular. Cars devoured vast quantities of oil. Geologists searched the country for new sources of this precious fuel. In 1922, oil fields were discovered in San Juan County in northwestern New Mexico. Soon more oil wells went into operation at Artesia in the southeastern part of the state. Oil brought money, roads, and more people than ever into once-quiet New Mexico.

Hard Times and Strange Secrets

New Mexico was a charming getaway for people with money and education. But opportunities were scarce for most native-born New Mexicans. Few jobs were available in remote villages or on the reservations where many Native Americans lived. During the 1930s, the United States plunged into a terrible economic depression. Thousands of New Mexicans moved to Albuquerque in search of work. Many lived in tents and tar-paper shacks on the edge of the city. They walked the streets every day, looking for jobs that did not exist. Some survived only by accepting help from government welfare programs.

The Great Depression ended in 1939. But the nation faced another crisis with the outbreak of World War II. Young men from New Mexico hurried to enlist in the armed services. Hundreds of

them never saw their home state again. In the first months of the war, New Mexico had more casualties than any other state.

Since the 1920s, the Los Alamos Ranch School had been a boarding school for boys. When the school suddenly shut its doors in 1942, few people gave the event much thought. They did not know that the school had been purchased by agents of the U.S. gov-

The Los Alamos Ranch School, which became the site for a top-secret military project

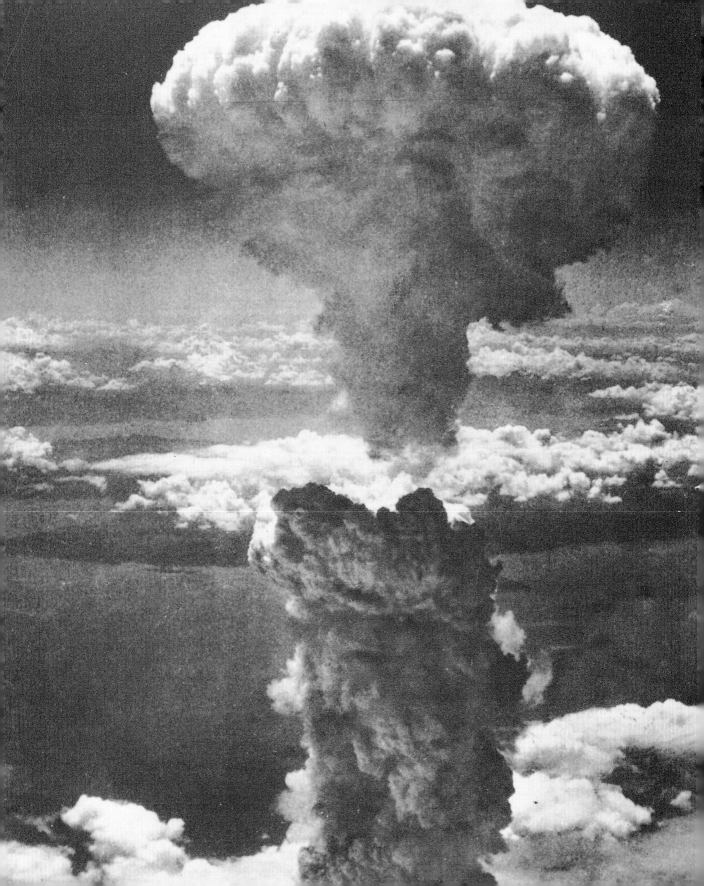

ernment. Its remote desert location made it the perfect site for a top-secret military program.

In 1943, hundreds of scientists arrived at the former school. Sentries guarded the gates. The scientists could not receive visitors or even phone calls. All of their mail went to a post office box.

For sixteen months, the scientists worked at Los Alamos. On the morning of July 16, 1945, project leaders huddled in a bunker north of the town of Alamogordo. They waited in breathless expectation. Suddenly a ball of orange fire leaped into the sky. A dreadful roar shook the very earth. Physicist J. Robert Oppenheimer watched the blast in awe. He murmured a line from an ancient Hindu text: "I am become death, destroyer of worlds."

The scientists at Los Alamos had created the world's first atomic bomb. Weeks after the blast at Alamogordo, the United States used this devastating new weapon on the Japanese cities of Hiroshima and Nagasaki. The atomic bomb brought World War II to an end. But it launched the world into a frightening new age. Terrible weapons of mass destruction now rested in human hands.

Reaching to the Future

If you drive down a New Mexico highway on a winter day, you will notice many cars with ski racks on their roofs. Probably they are headed for Taos, Angel Fire, or one of the state's other ski resorts. As New Mexico's roads improved in the 1950s, investors saw the chance to develop resorts for out-of-state visitors. Tourism expanded rapidly to become a mainstay of New Mexico's economy.

Tourism helped spur New Mexico's growth in the decades

The Desert of Glass

White Sands Missile Range is usually off-limits to the public. But twice a year a military escort leads visitors through the gates. Here, on a fateful day in 1945, scientists set off the world's first nuclear explosion. The blast was so powerful that it broke windows more than 100 miles (160 km) away. The intense heat melted desert sand and fused it into glass. ▪

Opposite: The mushroom cloud that resulted from the atomic bomb dropped on Nagasaki during World War II

Concern for the Underprivileged

Dionisio (Dennis) Chavez (1888–1962) was the first Mexican-American to serve in the U.S. Senate. He was born in Los Chavez, New Mexico, and was elected to the U.S. House of Representatives in 1931. He held a seat in the Senate from 1935 until his death, being reelected five times. Chavez never forgot his Latino heritage. During his long Senate career, he worked tirelessly on behalf of the nation's Native American and Hispanic minorities. He is remembered as a chief architect of the U.S. Fair Employment Practices Commission, which worked to end racial discrimination in employment. Chavez's statue stands in the U.S. Capitol, a tribute to his service to New Mexico and to the nation. ■

after World War II. But the state emerged as far more than a playground for visitors. The federal government did not close its laboratory at Los Alamos when the war was over. The once-secret community of scientists became a nationally famous atomic research facility. Other research stations opened in and around Albuquerque. The military tested weapons at White Sands Missile Range, where the first atomic bomb exploded in 1945. By the 1960s, New Mexico claimed more residents with doctoral degrees (Ph.D.s) than any other state.

Research and tourism brought billions of dollars into New Mexico. Yet little of this wealth trickled down to the state's poorest inhabitants. Jobs and services remained limited in rural areas. Conditions were especially grim on the state's American Indian reservations. Tribal leaders and government officials worked to improve education and health care for Native Americans. In the 1990s, several New Mexico reservations opened gaming casinos as tribal-run businesses. The casinos created jobs and brought income to the tribes.

After World War II, the United States and the Soviet Union were locked in a forty-year struggle known as the cold war. No shots were fired, but each nation built up its defenses to be prepared for trouble. In 1990, the Soviet Union's government collapsed and the cold war came to an end. The U.S. government cut spending on weapons research. In New Mexico, military bases closed and laboratories scaled down their projects.

New Mexicans shifted their attention to the computer industry. Companies began producing computer chips and other electronic

Many military bases and laboratories in New Mexico closed, making way for the computer industry.

components. Private corporations took over some federal research centers such as Sandia National Laboratories in Albuquerque. Weapons research did not disappear from the state. But research extended into such fields as medicine, genetics, and telecommunications.

In the late 1990s, New Mexico moved still farther away from dependence on government contracts. Governor Gary Johnson worked to put more and more industries into private hands. Johnson was fond of saying, "If private enterprise prospers, New Mexico prospers."

Despite its involvement with high-tech industries, New Mexico did not forget the richness of its past. The state worked to preserve its Anasazi ruins and old Spanish missions. In the 1990s, an ambitious project hired New Mexico teens to restore crumbling eighteenth- and nineteenth-century churches. The young people learned to make adobe, the material the Native Americans and later the Spaniards used for making bricks. First the teens mixed straw into wet clay. Then they shaped the clay into bricks and set them out to dry. Like the Anasazi who had lived 800 years before, they dried their adobe bricks in the sun of the high plateau.

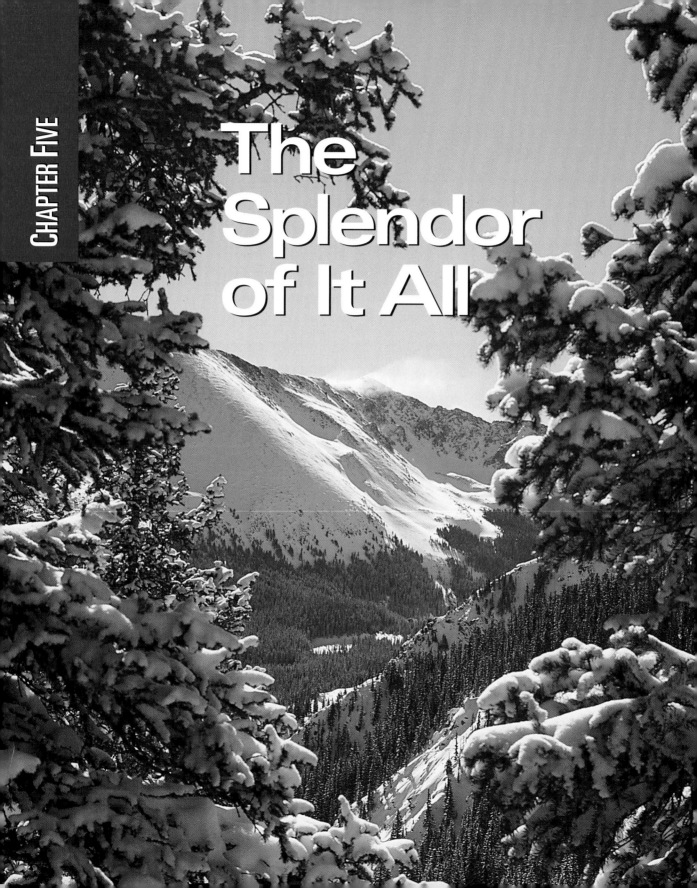

CHAPTER FIVE

The Splendor of It All

Sunset across New Mexico's Florida Mountains

"All those mornings I went with a hoe along the ditch to the canyon at the ranch and stood in the fierce, proud silence of the Rockies, to look far over the depths to the blue mountains away in Arizona, . . . with the sagebrush desert sweeping gray-blue in between, . . . the vast amphitheater of lofty, indomitable desert sweeping round to the Sangre de Cristo Mountains to the east and coming up flush with the pine-dotted foothills of the Rockies. What splendor! Only the tawny eagle could really sail out into the splendor of it all!"—British author D. H. Lawrence, who lived near Taos in the early 1920s.

The Lay of the Land

With its mountains, canyons, high plateaus, and flat-topped mesas, New Mexico is a showcase of natural wonders. Every corner of the state offers something dazzling and unique. Few other states can claim such extraordinary scenic beauty.

New Mexico lies in the southwestern part of the United States.

Opposite: The mountains of northern New Mexico

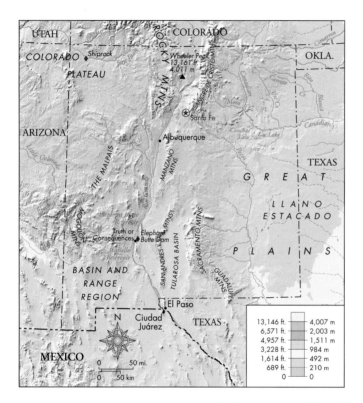

New Mexico's topography

On a map, it is roughly square in shape. It is bordered by Arizona to the west, Colorado to the north, and Oklahoma and Texas to the east. Texas shares most of its southern border as well. The "boot-heel" section, an extension off the southwestern corner of the square, touches Mexico. Sprawling across 121,598 square miles (314,937 sq km), New Mexico is the fifth-largest state in the Union. Only Alaska, Texas, California, and Montana are bigger.

Though New Mexico has little rainfall, it has several rivers that provide water for irrigation. Among them are the Pecos, the Canadian, the San Juan, and the Gila. The Rio Grande is the longest and most important river in the state. It flows south from Colorado, cutting New Mexico almost in half.

Where Four Corners Meet

The northwestern corner of New Mexico is often referred to as the Four Corners region. This is the only spot in the United States where the corners of four states come together. It would actually be possible for you to crouch on the ground with your right foot in New Mexico, your left foot in Arizona, your right hand in Colorado, and your left hand in Utah. The Four Corners region is one of the most remote parts of New Mexico and lies within the Navajo Reservation. Many Anasazi ruins are preserved in this region. ■

The Elephant Butte Dam crosses the Rio Grande near the town of Truth or Consequences. It forms Elephant Butte Reservoir, the largest lake in the state. The name *Rio Grande* means "big river" in Spanish. For this reason, the Rio Grande is never called the Rio Grande River. That would be calling it the "Big River River."

The Rio Grande, the state's longest and most important river

Elephant Butte Reservoir is the largest lake in New Mexico.

Truth or Consequences

In 1950, Ralph Edwards, the host of the popular radio game show *Truth or Consequences*, dreamed up a unique gimmick to publicize his program. He searched the nation for a town willing to be renamed in honor of his show. Hot Springs, New Mexico, accepted the challenge and changed its name to Truth or Consequences. The name change brought a surge of publicity to the town, which is a health spa and retirement center. Today, most locals shorten the name to T or C. ■

The Staked Plain

Perhaps the name comes from the stakes early ranchers used for marking their land claims. Perhaps it refers to the tall yucca plants that jut like stakes from the flat land. To this day, no one is certain how the *Llano Estacado,* or Staked Plain, got its name. ■

The eastern third of New Mexico is a high, rolling grassland. This region is an extension of the Great Plains that stretch across the central United States. Much of New Mexico's plain is devoted to cattle grazing. The flat land south of the Canadian River is called the *Llano Estacado,* or Staked Plain.

As you head west, the high plain breaks into rugged, mountainous terrain. New Mexico's tallest mountains, the Rockies, are in the north-central part of the state. Many of these peaks are capped with snow. The highest point in the state, Wheeler Peak, is in the Rockies. It stands 13,161 feet (4,011 m) above sea level.

To the south and west the

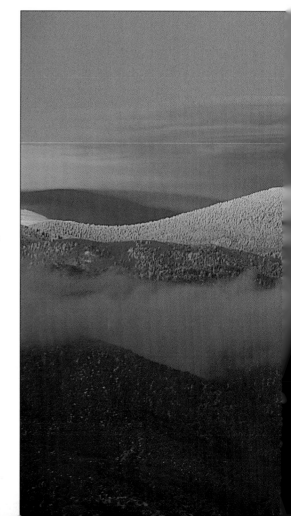

Rockies give way to a series of lower mountain ranges. The *Sangre de Cristo* (Blood of Christ) Mountains stand on the eastern side of the Rio Grande. To the west of the river are the Jemez and Nacimiento Ranges. Farther south the Rio Grande and its branches run through the Mogollon, Organ, Guadalupe, Sacramento, and San Andres Mountains. Geographers call the south-central and southwestern part of New Mexico the Basin and Range region. Between the mountains lie dry, bowl-like valleys, or basins. The largest of these is the Tularosa Basin between the Organ and Sacramento Mountains.

A light blanket of snow on the Sangre de Cristo Mountains

The badlands, a region that can appear bleak and lifeless

Northwestern New Mexico is part of a large land region known as the Colorado Plateau. It includes a portion of the Sonora Desert, most of which lies in Arizona. Northwestern New Mexico is a dramatic landscape of deep canyons, cliffs, and mesas. The Colorado Plateau embraces a desolate 40-mile (64-km) strip of lava flows and craters from extinct volcanoes. This area is known as the Malpais, or badlands. The Malpais is so bleak that it looks like the lifeless surface of the moon.

High and Dry

Now and then as you drive down a New Mexico highway, you may see a swirl of dust dancing along the roadside. These "dust devils" are born when the wind gathers the powder-dry topsoil into a

New Mexico's Geographical Features

Total area; rank	121,598 sq. mi. (314,937 sq km); 5th
Land; rank	121,364 sq. mi. (314,331 sq km); 5th
Water; rank	234 sq. mi. (606 sq km); 47th
***Inland water;* rank**	234 sq. mi. (606 sq km); 44th
Geographic center	Torrance, 12 miles (19 km) southwest of Willard
Highest point	Wheeler Peak, 13,161 feet (4,011 m)
Lowest point	Red Bluff Reservoir, 2,842 feet (866 m)
Largest city	Albuquerque
Population; rank	1,819,046 (2000 census); 36th
Record high temperature	116°F (47°C) at Orogrande on July 14, 1934, and at Artesia on June 29, 1918
Record low temperature	–50°F (–46°C) at Gavilan, near Lindrith, on February 1, 1951
Average July temperature	74°F (23°C)
Average January temperature	34°F (1°C)
Average annual precipitation	13 inches (33 cm)

Shiprock

One of the most striking features of the Colorado Plateau is a steep hill known as Shiprock. The hill gets its name because it resembles a ship with billowing sails. Shiprock soars 1,678 feet (512 m) above the surrounding plateau. ■

Much of southern New Mexico is desert and gets little rain each year.

twisting, funnel-shaped cloud. In this land of little rain, dust devils are a common sight.

Much of southern New Mexico is parched desert country. Winters are mild, but summer weather can be brutally hot. The sun blazes down during the day, but at nightfall, temperatures plummet. On average, southern New Mexico gets less than 10 inches (25 cm) of precipitation per year.

The mountains of northern New Mexico receive about 20 inches (51 cm) of annual precipitation. Snowfall is often heavy. Compared with other parts of the country, however, northern New Mexico is still very dry. New Jersey, for example, has 46 inches (117 cm) of precipitation a year.

When it does rain in New Mexico, it rains hard. In a heavy downpour, the bone-dry earth cannot absorb the water fast enough. Runoff turns every gully into a rushing stream. Flash floods pose a serious threat to livestock and to humans.

Thunderstruck

Each year more people are killed by lightning in New Mexico than in any other state. The naturalist Aldo Leopold once wrote, "The explosions [of thunder] are fearsome enough, but more so are the smoking slivers of stone that sing past your ear when the bolt crashes into a rimrock. Still more so are the splinters that fly when a bolt explodes a pine. I remember one gleaming white one, fifteen feet long, that stabbed deep into the earth at my feet and stood there humming like a tuning fork." ■

Where the Deer and the Antelope Play

When the first Spaniards reached New Mexico, the eastern plains were alive with deer, pronghorn antelope, and vast herds of bison. Today, only the mule deer is still common. The bison have disappeared from New Mexico, and the pronghorn is a protected species. The fastest animal in North America, the pronghorn has been known to reach a speed of 44 mph (71 km) per hour.

The wail of the coyote is a familiar sound in rural New Mexico. Ranchers have waged war on the coyote for centuries because it kills lambs and young calves. But the coyote is clever enough to avoid most traps and poisons. It also learns not to give away its presence by howling when it lives close to a city or town. Black bears and cougars, or mountain lions, are New

Mule deer are a common sight in the eastern plains of New Mexico.

The Underground Palace

In 1901, a cowboy named James White saw thousands of bats streaming from an opening in the ground near Carlsbad in southeastern New Mexico. The bats revealed the entrance to an extraordinary maze of underground rooms and tunnels. These caves were formed over millions of years as water carved its way through limestone bedrock. The Carlsbad Caverns were declared a national park in 1930.

Today, Carlsbad Caverns is an immensely popular tourist attraction, drawing visitors from around the world. Visitors follow a winding 3-mile (5-km) trail among dazzling mineral formations called stalagmites and stalactites. Stalagmites rise up from the cavern floor, and stalactites hang down from above. It is easy to get the names of the two formations mixed up. Just remember that stalactites hold tight to the ceiling.

The chambers in Carlsbad Caverns have been given an array of intriguing names. These include Whale's Mouth, King's Palace, and Hall of the Giants. Perhaps the most spectacular chamber in the caverns is simply called the Big Room. Its arching roof soars 256 feet (78 m) high. The room is so vast that it could hold fourteen Astrodomes.

Many areas of the caverns are strictly off-limits to visitors. Among them are the nesting chambers of Carlsbad's immense colony of Mexican free-tailed bats. Carlsbad Caverns is home to about 300,000 of these small, graceful creatures. Every evening from May to November the bats fly from the caves in a cloud that looks like curling smoke. The bats have a voracious appetite for mosquitoes and other insects, and are highly beneficial to humans in the region. ▨

Mexico's only other large predators. Both try to avoid contact with humans and stay in the state's most remote areas.

Among New Mexico's smaller mammals are ground squirrels, opossums, skunks, and jackrabbits. The jackrabbit is more than twice the size of the common eastern cottontail. It is often seen bounding along New Mexico roadways. The pika, or rock rabbit, lives on the upper reaches of the mountains. During the summer, it gathers grasses and dries them in the sun. It lives on this hay through the long, hard winter.

About 25 percent of New Mexico's land is covered with forests. The Gila National Forest is the largest of seven national forests in the state. Forest trees include cottonwood, scrub oak, spruce, juniper, and ponderosa pine. The piñon pine is one of New

The jackrabbit is among the state's smaller mammals.

In Search of the Jackelope

Many New Mexico artists make and sell tiny ceramic figures of coyotes, deer, bears, and other animals found in the state. Visitors love to browse the shops, selecting a few of these figures to take home as souvenirs. Every now and then the visitor notices a strange, unfamiliar creature among the others. It has the body, tail, and long hind legs of a rabbit. But from its head springs a pair of branching horns. Straight-faced, New Mexicans explain that this is the jackelope, a cross between the pronghorn and the jackrabbit. Though jackelopes can be found in most New Mexico souvenir shops, none has ever yet been captured alive. ■

New Mexico's parks and forests

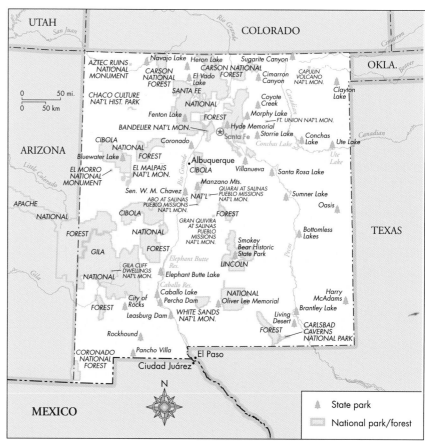

Spending time in the Gila National Forest

Mexico's best-loved trees. To many New Mexicans, the fragrance of piñon smoke from a winter fireplace is the smell of home.

Many kinds of cacti grow in New Mexico's desert basins. Tumbleweeds, though not native to the state, are now common in semi-arid and grassy areas. In the fall, the large, round tops of the tumbleweed dry and tear away from the stems. The wind bounces these spiky balls over the ground, scattering seeds far and wide. When a brushfire breaks out, tumbleweeds pose a serious hazard by spreading sparks as they roll.

"Only You Can Prevent Forest Fires!"

In 1950, firefighters rescued an orphaned bear cub after a forest fire near Capitan, New Mexico. The cub, named Smokey, was moved to the National Zoo in Washington, D.C. Smokey Bear became the "spokesman" for a nationwide fire prevention campaign. He appeared on billboards, in films, and in public service announcements on TV. In a gruff, bearlike voice, Smokey reminded his listeners, "Only you can prevent forest fires!" ■

CHAPTER SIX

Back Roads and Highways

New Mexico is not a state of large cities. Only Albuquerque has more than 100,000 people. Santa Fe, the state capital, is about one-third the size of such suburban communities as Evanston, Illinois, or White Plains, New York. Yet each of New Mexico's small cities and towns is rich in the traditions of the state's three cultures. All stand against the backdrop of New Mexico's extraordinary natural beauty.

Cattle ranching is the livelihood of many people who live in New Mexico's plains.

On the High Plains

Much of eastern New Mexico is a high, rolling plain, broken here and there by hills and mountain chains. Many people in this region raise horses and cattle. Others work in the petroleum business. Towns are few and widely scattered along lonely stretches of highway.

Southeastern New Mexico

The town of Hobbs nestles above the Texas border in New Mexico's oil and cattle country. It celebrates its cattle-ranching history at the

Opposite: A Santa Fe window

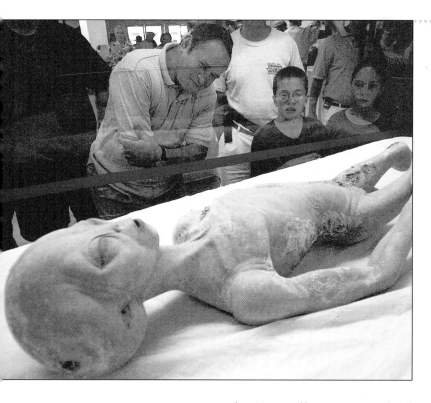

An "alien" at the International UFO Museum and Research Center in Roswell

Lea County Cowboy Hall of Fame and Western Heritage Center. This museum displays memorabilia from the cowboy days of the late nineteenth and early twentieth centuries. One exhibit contains archaeological findings of early humans who lived in the area.

A town of some 50,000 people, Roswell is southeastern New Mexico's largest community. It rises from the vast flat plain called the Llano Estacado. Roswell was once the home of Roswell Air Force Base. Most visitors, however, are more interested in flying objects of the unidentified variety. The International UFO Museum and Research Center and the UFO Enigma Museum make Roswell the UFO capital of the world. Both museums were inspired by the alleged

Visitors from Beyond

In July 1947, witnesses claimed that they saw a spaceship crash into the desert northwest of Roswell. Some even insisted they saw the bodies of three aliens. According to government investigators, the "flying saucer" was nothing but a crashed weather balloon. Such official denials only add fuel to the rumors. Today, UFO enthusiasts flock to Roswell from all over the world. But the only aliens they are likely to see are in museums or stenciled on the T-shirts and coffee mugs sold in Roswell's souvenir shops. ■

landing of an alien spacecraft at Roswell in 1947. The Roswell Museum and Art Center has seventeen galleries with Native American pottery, early Spanish armor, and modern paintings (including many works by the noted painter Georgia O'Keeffe.) The museum also includes a replica of the laboratory where Robert Goddard developed his liquid-fuel rockets.

Every Monday horse lovers gather in Clovis for the weekly horse auction. Clovis is home to the biggest horse and mule market in the United States. The auction is a wonderful place to see

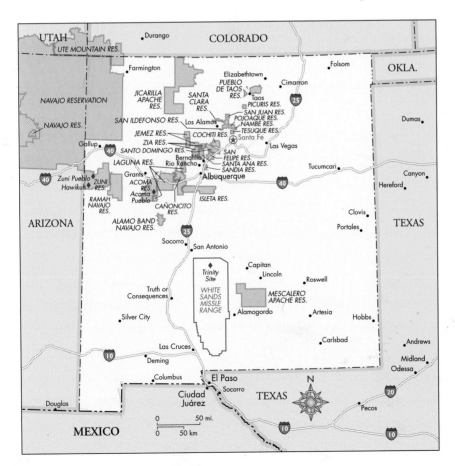

New Mexico's cities and interstates

Excavations at Black Water Draw

fast-talking horse traders at work and to admire some of the most splendid animals the West can produce.

Clovis has a special significance for archaeologists. Spear points found in the area, known as Clovis points, are evidence that people lived here more than 10,000 years ago. In 1932, a cowboy found several Clovis points and a number of mammoth bones in a gully called Black Water Draw. Today, spear points and other artifacts are on display at the Black Water Draw Museum.

As you head north, the eastern plain breaks into rolling hills. The town of Tucumcari is named after a nearby mountain, but no one knows for sure how the mountain got its name. The name may come from a Comanche word meaning "signal mountain," or it may come from an Apache legend about tragic lovers named Tocom and Cari. Tucumcari is a way station for truckers, tourists, and travelers of all kinds. It is a town of 6,000 people that boasts it has 2,000 motel rooms. An amazing assortment of collections

King of the Wild West

When he was a teenager, William Cody (1846–1917) worked as a horseback messenger on the Great Plains. Later he became a soldier and scout for the U.S. Army. Cody slaughtered thousands of bison to feed railroad crews. Some historians believe he deliberately wiped out the bison to destroy the food supply and nomadic way of life of the Native Americans. His bison hunting earned Cody the nickname Buffalo Bill.

As the Wild West disappeared, Cody gave it new life in a traveling stage show. Audiences thrilled to reenacted buffalo hunts, shootouts, and battles between white ranchers and Apaches in colorful war paint. Cody organized his first road show in 1883 while living at the St. James Hotel in Cimarron. ■

can be seen at the Tucumcari Historical Museum. There are spear points, saddles, antique cookware, and bins of rocks and gemstones.

Cimarron lies in the green foothills of the Rocky Mountains. Once a stop on the Taos branch of the Santa Fe Trail, this town is drenched in frontier legends. An 1876 newspaper reported, "Everything is quiet in Cimarron. Nobody has been killed in three days." Twenty-six cowboys were murdered in the St. James Hotel, built in 1849 and now fully restored. The tin ceiling in the lobby still has twenty bullet holes.

North-Central New Mexico

North-central New Mexico is the most densely populated section of the state. Its cities and towns lie in a beautiful landscape of mountains and rivers. The spellbinding scenery is one of the region's leading attractions.

Albuquerque is the state's economic and cultural center.

About one-third of all New Mexicans live in Albuquerque and the towns that cluster around it. Though Santa Fe is the state capital, Albuquerque is New Mexico's economic and cultural hub. It is home to the state's leading banks and businesses, and to the University of New Mexico, which has an enrollment of 24,000 students.

Albuquerque straddles the Rio Grande and lies among the Manzano and Sandia Mountains. The Sandia Tramway lifts visitors to a snowcapped peak 10,678 feet (3,257 m) above sea level. Neighborhoods of houses and apartments have replaced the ranches that once surrounded Albuquerque. Many of these neighborhoods still carry the names of the old Spanish ranches: Los Griegos, Duranes, and Los Poblanos. Albuquerque's growth was spurred by the arrival of the Santa Fe Railroad in 1884. With the railroad boom, Albuquerque rapidly eclipsed Santa Fe to become New Mexico's most important city.

Albuquerque's Old Town section is the site of the city's original Spanish settlement. San Felipe de Neri Church was built there in 1706, the year the city was founded. The Albuquerque Museum in Old Town traces the city's three-century history through maps, paintings, and documentary films.

Life-sized models of dinosaurs guard the entrance to the Albuquerque Museum of Natural History and Science. Exhibits of fossils, early human artifacts, plants, and animals focus on New Mexico and the Southwest. Visitors can even walk through a model of a live volcano. Another fascinating museum is the Indian Pueblo Cultural Center. A series of dioramas details the lifestyles of the Hopi, Zuni, Jemez, and other distinct Pueblo groups before the arrival of Europeans. Other displays depict Indian life today. One diorama even includes a camera-toting tourist.

Heading west from Albuquerque you find yourself in a landscape of canyons and mesas. Perched atop one such mesa is Acoma Pueblo, where about thirty families live without electricity or running water. An ancient stone stairway twists its way up the rock face. People have lived here since about 1075, making Acoma the oldest town in the United States.

Santa Fe, New Mexico's state capital, calls itself the "City Different." With only 62,000 people, it is one of the smallest state capitals in the country. The older buildings are made of adobe, and the newer ones have an adobe look. It is sometimes said that Santa Fe houses come in four dozen shades of brown. Sante Fe has long paid

Sante Fe has more than 250 art galleries.

homage to the arts. It overflows with galleries and hosts a world-class opera festival each summer.

The center of Santa Fe is the square, or plaza. Here Spanish soldiers practiced marching as early as 1610. Native American craftspeople spread blankets under the plaza's porticos and sell their work—baskets, leather sandals, pottery, and exquisite jewelry of silver and turquoise. On the north side of the plaza, the Palace of the Governors now houses the Museum of New Mexico. Its displays chart the influences of Native Americans, Spaniards, and Anglos on the capital. The palace is part of the Museum of New

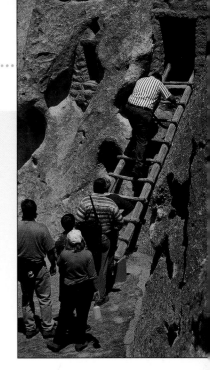

Scaling the Cliffs

At Bandelier National Monument, daring hikers can climb a series of wooden ladders to an Anasazi dwelling 140 feet above the canyon floor. Bandelier includes 60 miles (97 km) of trails in a 46-square-mile (119-sq-km) park south of Los Alamos.

Bandelier National Monument was named in honor of Adolf Francis Alphonse Bandelier (1840–1914), a Swiss-born naturalist who explored the area in the 1880s. From 1880 until 1886, Bandelier lived with the region's Pueblo people. He wrote several scholarly reports about Native American life. His experiences in New Mexico also inspired him to write a novel, *The Delight Makers*. ■

Mexico complex that also includes the Museum of Fine Arts, the Museum of Indian Arts and Culture, and the Museum of International Folk Art.

Northwest of Santa Fe lies Los Alamos, the one-time "secret city." Today, Los Alamos National Laboratory is a thriving center for atomic research. Photos, models, and hands-on exhibits at the Bradbury Science Museum showcase the laboratory's work. One of the museum's treasures is a 1939 letter from Albert Einstein to President Franklin D. Roosevelt. In the letter, Einstein urges research into the use of uranium to create a powerful new weapon. Yet he warns that such research might have dire consequences for the future of humankind.

Set in the mountains 70 miles (113 km) north of Santa Fe, Taos is a town of glorious views and spectacular sunsets. About 10 percent of its residents are artists, writers, or musicians. The work of many local artists is on display at the Van Vechten–Lineberry Taos Art Museum, opened in 1995. At Taos Pueblo, just north of the

Bent Street in
scenic Taos

town, some families still live in traditional adobe apartments, climbing wooden ladders to reach their doors.

Mountains and Deserts

Towns are scarce in many parts of western and southern New Mexico. These sprawling regions are startlingly beautiful, though they can be inhospitable to human inhabitants. But here and there in the mountains and desert basins, hardy souls have established towns and coaxed them to survive.

If the streets and storefronts of Gallup look familiar, perhaps you have seen them in one of the many western movies filmed here in the 1930s and 1940s. Gallup lies near the Arizona border on the southern edge of the vast Navajo reservation. At the annual McKinley County Fair, Navajo, Apache, and Pueblo parade through town

The Shalako Dance

Zuni Pueblo prepares all year for the Shalako Dance, held in late November or early December. Special houses are built for the six shalakos, gods who can bring rain and grant fertility. The shalakos appear at sundown and enter the houses that have been made ready for them. The gods are represented by carved masks that tower 10 feet (3 m) high. The shalako masks have large, beaked noses and glossy black hair some 5 feet (1.5 m) long. Within each mask, a man works mechanical controls to move the great mouth.

For twenty-four hours, the shalakos are honored with a glorious feast. A series of dances reenacts Zuni myths about the creation of the earth, animals, and human beings. The dancing is accompanied by a cycle of hypnotic chants.

The shalako festival is open to the public. The Zuni ask only that visitors be quiet and respectful and that they refrain from using cameras. From the end of the festival until the winter solstice (December 21), the Zuni practice a series of sacred rituals to ensure prosperity in the coming year. These ceremonies are closed to outsiders. ■

in traditional masks and headdresses. A highlight of the fair is the All-Indian Rodeo, where Native Americans rope steers and ride wild broncos.

The largest pueblo in New Mexico, with over 6,000 residents, is Zuni Pueblo, which lies a little south of Gallup. Today's pueblo is 12 miles (19 km) from Hawikuh, the village Marcos de Niza mistook for a city of gold in 1539. The Zuni still preserve many aspects of their traditional non-Christian religion. Medicine men and women perform rituals to bring rain, to make crops grow, and to heal the sick.

Only an hour from the border with Mexico, Las Cruces has a

New Mexico's Stargazer

In 1905, an astronomer named Percival Lowell noticed irregularities in the orbit of the planet Uranus. Lowell believed that Uranus must be affected by the gravitational pull of a more distant planet that was unknown to science. For the next twenty-five years, dedicated astronomers at Lowell Observatory in Arizona searched the skies. At last, in 1930, a young Lowell astronomer named Clyde W. Tombaugh (1906–1997) made headlines around the world. Tombaugh had spotted Pluto, the ninth planet in the solar system.

A few years after his groundbreaking discovery, Tombaugh left Arizona and settled in New Mexico. Tombaugh taught astronomy for many years at New Mexico State University in Las Cruces. ▪

rich Mexican atmosphere. The name *Las Cruces* means "the crosses." During colonial times, Native Americans sometimes ambushed Spanish travelers in the nearby mountain passes. Crosses later marked the graves of those who were killed. Las Cruces is New Mexico's second-largest city and is home to New Mexico State University. It has two charming historic districts and a fine natural history museum.

Alamogordo stands like a courageous outpost in the stark Tularosa Basin. Around it spreads a bleached landscape of sand and cacti. The nearby White Sands Missile Range is the region's biggest

A plaza in Las Cruces

employer. Alamogordo's Space Center is a wonderful place to study the history of space exploration. The center houses the International Space Hall of Fame, which preserves memorabilia from U.S. and Soviet space travels. The Clyde W. Tombaugh Space Theater offers films, light shows, and a planetarium.

Rockets are on display at the International Space Hall of Fame.

CHAPTER SEVEN

Under the Zia Sun

The New Mexico state capitol in Santa Fe is one of the newest capitol buildings in the country. It was constructed in 1966 and extensively remodeled in 1992. Visitors often remark that the capitol is ultramodern. It is a circular building with four extensions, or wings. Actually, the building's form reaches back to New Mexico's prehistory. The capitol was designed to look like the sun sign of the Zia Pueblo people. To the Zia, the sun is a symbol of happiness and prosperity.

New Mexico's modern state capitol

The Law of the People

New Mexico still operates under its original state constitution. This body of laws was adopted in 1911, a few months before New Mexico joined the union in January 1912. Although the constitution has never been completely rewritten, it has been amended, or changed, about one hundred times.

Several special sections of the constitution protect the rights of New Mexico's Spanish-speaking minority. They ensure that Spanish-speaking New Mexicans have full voting rights and equal rights to an education. Under the constitution, all laws passed by the state legislature must be published in both English and Spanish.

Opposite: A hot-air balloon featuring the Zia sun

The interior of the
state capitol

Like the federal government, New Mexico's government is divided into three branches. The executive branch, or office of the governor, makes sure that the laws are carried out. The legislative branch makes and repeals laws. The judicial branch, or court system, interprets the laws.

New Mexicans elect their governor to a four-year term. The governor can succeed himself or herself, serving not more than two terms in a row. Other elected officials in the executive branch are the lieutenant governor, secretary of state, attorney general, treasurer, auditor, and commissioner of public lands. Ten members of the board of education are elected to serve six-year terms. The gov-

New Mexico's Governors

Name	Party	Term	Name	Party	Term
William C. McDonald	Dem.	1912–1917	Edwin L. Mechem	Rep.	1951–1955
Ezequiel C. de Baca	Dem.	1917	John F. Simms	Dem.	1955–1957
Washington E. Lindsey	Rep.	1917–1919	Edwin L. Mechem	Rep.	1957–1959
Octaviano A. Larrazolo	Rep.	1919–1921	John Burroughs	Dem.	1959–1961
Merritt C. Mechem	Rep.	1921–1923	Edwin L. Mechem	Rep.	1961–1963
James F. Hinkle	Dem.	1923–1925	Jack M. Campbell	Dem.	1963–1967
Arthur T. Hannett	Dem.	1925–1927	David F. Cargo	Rep.	1967–1971
Richard C. Dillon	Rep.	1927–1931	Bruce King	Dem.	1971–1975
Arthur Seligman	Dem.	1931–1933	Jerry Apodaca	Dem.	1975–1979
A. W. Hockenhull	Rep.	1933–1935	Bruce King	Dem.	1979–1983
Clyde Tingley	Dem.	1935–1939	Toney Anaya	Dem.	1983–1987
John E. Miles	Dem.	1939–1943	Garrey Carruthers	Rep.	1987–1991
John J. Dempsey	Dem.	1943–1947	Bruce King	Dem.	1991–1995
Thomas J. Mabry	Dem.	1947–1951	Gary E. Johnson	Rep.	1995–

The State Flag and Seal

New Mexico's state flag (above) shows the Zia sun sign in red against a gold background. The sun sign is a circle with four points radiating from it. To the Zia people, the circle represents prosperity and happiness. Four is a sacred number, related to the four directions and the four seasons. Crimson and gold were the colors of Spain at the time of the early Spanish explorations in North America. This flag, honoring the Native American and Spanish influences in New Mexico, was adopted in 1925.

The state seal (right) shows a large eagle shielding a smaller one. The image represents the annexation of New Mexico by the United States. The state seal was adopted in 1912, the year New Mexico joined the union. ■

The New Mexico legislature consists of the senate and the house of representatives.

ernor appoints the board members of such state institutions as psychiatric hospitals and the schools for the deaf and blind. He or she has the right to veto, or turn down, any bill voted in by the legislature.

The state legislature of New Mexico has two sections, or houses. The upper house, or senate, has forty-two members who are elected to four-year terms. The lower house, or house of representatives, has seventy members. Representatives only serve two-year terms. The legislature meets for sixty days in odd-numbered years and for thirty days in even-numbered years. The governor can call a special session at any time, or the legislators themselves can ask for a special session.

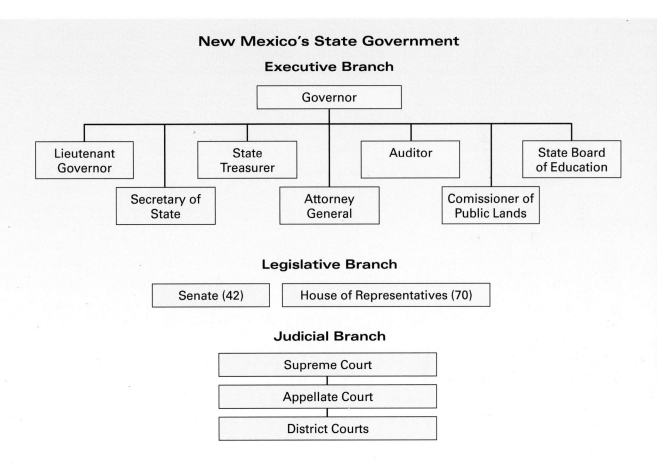

New Mexico's State Government

Executive Branch

Governor

- Lieutenant Governor
- Secretary of State
- State Treasurer
- Attorney General
- Auditor
- Comissioner of Public Lands
- State Board of Education

Legislative Branch

Senate (42)   House of Representatives (70)

Judicial Branch

Supreme Court

Appellate Court

District Courts

A person accused of committing a crime in New Mexico is usually first tried in a district court. District courts are held in each of the state's thirty-three counties. If the person is found guilty, he or she can appeal the case to the appellate court. The highest court in the state is the supreme court, with five justices elected to eight-year terms.

Most counties in New Mexico are run by an elected board of commissioners. Only Los Alamos County has a somewhat differ-

New Mexico's State Symbols

State bird: Roadrunner The roadrunner (left) is a member of the cuckoo family. It prefers a semi-desert environment, where it lives on insects, lizards, and small snakes. A poor flier, the roadrunner is often seen racing along beside New Mexico highways.

State fish: Cutthroat trout The cutthroat trout is a prized game fish that may weigh up to 3 pounds (1.4 kg) or more. It gets its name because it has a bright red streak beneath its lower jaw. The fish looks as though its throat has been cut.

State dinosaur: Coelophysis Fossils of the 6-foot (1.8-m)-long coelophysis were first discovered in New Mexico's Tularosa Basin. A fully assembled skeleton is on view at the Albuquerque Museum of Natural History and Science.

State tree: Piñon pine The piñon is a small, bushy pine that grows to a height of 20 to 30 feet (6 to 9 m). Its dried branches are often burned for firewood. The seeds of the piñon, known as pine nuts, are used in New Mexican cooking.

State vegetables: Chile pepper and pinto bean These two vegetables are staples of New Mexican cooking. Pinto beans can be boiled or refried. Hot chile peppers can add spice to any dish. Before the arrival of Europeans, chiles were the only source of vitamin C for the native New Mexicans.

State flower: Yucca The yucca (bottom left) is a tall plant with a woody stem. Clusters of white, bell-shaped flowers grow from a stalk that springs from the plant's center. Native Americans discovered that yucca flowers are edible. So is the fruit, which appears later in the season.

State gem: Turquoise Prized for centuries by Native Americans, turquoise is a blue or greenish gemstone (below). Many turquoise deposits are found in New Mexico's volcanic soil. New Mexican jewelry-makers often set a glittering turquoise against a contrasting background of silver. ■

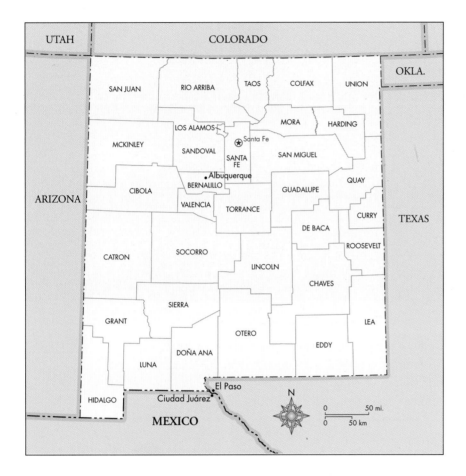

New Mexico's counties

ent system. Its affairs are controlled by a body called the city-county council. Towns in New Mexico are governed either by a mayor and council or by a city manager and board of commissioners.

Within New Mexico, the Pueblo, Navajo, and Apache function as separate self-governing nations. Each of the nineteen Pueblo communities, known as pueblos, elects its own governor. These governors work together in the All-Indian Pueblo Council. The Apache have a tribal council headed by an elected president

The state's breathtaking scenery was one of the inspirations for the song "O Fair New Mexico."

"O Fair New Mexico"

Under a sky of azure, where balmy breezes blow,
Kissed by the golden sunshine, is Nuevo Méjico.
Home of the Montezuma, with fiery heart aglow,
State of the deeds historic, is Nuevo Méjico.

Chorus:
O fair New Mexico, we love, we love you so,
Our hearts with pride o'erflow, no matter where we go,
O fair New Mexico, we love you, we love you so,
The grandest state to know, New Mexico.
Rugged and high sierras, with deep canyons below,
Dotted with fertile valleys, is Nuevo Méjico.
Fields full of sweet alfalfa, richest perfumes bestow,
State of apple blossoms, is Nuevo Méjico.
Days that are full of heart-dreams, nights when the moon hangs low,
Beaming its benediction, o'er Nuevo Méjico.
Land with its bright mañana [tomorrow], coming through weal and woe,
State of our esperanza [hope] is Nuevo Méjico. ■

New Mexico's State Songs

New Mexico has two state songs, one in English and one in Spanish. "O Fair New Mexico," words and music by Elizabeth Garrett, was adopted in 1917. "Así Es Nuevo Méjico," words and music by Amadeo Lucero, was adopted in 1971. ■

"Así Es Nuevo Méjico" ("Thus Is New Mexico")

Un canto que traigo muy dentro del
  alma
Lo canto a mi estado, mi tierra natal.
De flores dorada mi tierra encantada
De lindas mujeres, que no tiene igual.

Chorus:
Así es Nuevo Méjico
Así es esta tierra del sol
De sierras y valles, de tierras
  frutales
Así es Nuevo Méjico.
El negro, el hispano, el anglo, y el
  indio,
todos son tus hijos, todos por igual.
Tus pueblos, y aldeas, mi tierra encan-
  tada
De lindas mujeres que no tiene igual.
El Río del Norte que es el Río Grande
Sus aguas corrientes fluyen hasta el
  mar,
Y riegan tus campos
Mi tierra encantada de lindas mujeres
Que no tiene igual.
Tus campos se visten de flores de
  mayo,
De lindos colores que Dios les dotó
Tus pájaros cantan, mi tierra encantada,
Sus trinos de amores al ser celestial.
Mi tierra encantada de historia bañada
Tan linda, tan bella, sin comparación.
Te rindo homenaje, te rindo cariño
Soldado valiente, te rinde su amor.

One song I carry deep within
  me,
I sing it of my state, my native land.
My enchanted land golden with flowers,
With lovely women, it has no equal.

Chorus:
Thus is New Mexico,
Thus is this land of the sun,
Of mountains and valleys, of fruitful
  lands,
Thus is New Mexico.
The black, the Hispanic, the Anglo, and
  the Indian,
They are your children, one and all.
Your towns and villages, my enchanted
  land
Of lovely women, it has no equal.
The Northern River, the Rio Grande,
Its running waters flow to the
  sea,
And water your fields,
My enchanted land of lovely women
That has no equal.
Your flowering fields can be seen in
  May,
Bright with the colors God gave them,
Your birds sing, my enchanted land,
Their trills of love to the Celestial Being.
My enchanted land drenched in history,
So lovely, so beautiful, beyond compare.
I give you homage, I give you love,
Brave soldier, I give you love.

and vice president. The Navajo Nation elects a tribal council headed by a chairperson. In addition to electing tribal leaders, Native Americans have the right to vote in all state and national elections.

Where Does the Money Go?

Every time New Mexicans go to the store, a state sales tax is added to the cost of their purchases. They also pay taxes on their personal income. Taxes provide about half of New Mexico's funding, or revenue. Most of the rest comes from Washington, D.C., through federal grants and other government programs.

State taxes pay for the construction of highways as well as other projects.

A Leader in Diplomacy

In 1982, New Mexicans elected Bill Richardson (1947–) to represent them in the U.S. Congress. On more than one occasion, Richardson was called upon to help New Mexicans who were being held hostage overseas. He found that he had a flair for negotiating with foreign officials. Soon his aid was being enlisted on behalf of people from other states as well.

During his years in Congress, Richardson traveled to Burma, Haiti, North Korea, and Iraq to negotiate for U.S. citizens who were in trouble. In 1997, President Bill Clinton appointed Richardson to serve as U.S. ambassador to the United Nations. In this role, he put his skill for diplomacy to excellent use. The following year, 1998, Clinton appointed Richardson to fill the post of secretary of energy. ■

What does New Mexico do with all this money? State revenue helps to pay for highways, hospitals, libraries, and museums. It maintains forty state parks and five state monuments. The biggest expenditure in New Mexico's budget is education. In 1996, New Mexico spent $3,500 per elementary and high school student. This figure is fairly low compared to the expenditure for education in other states. New Mexico ranks only fortieth among the states in dollars spent per pupil per year.

CHAPTER EIGHT

Dollars
and Cents

anta Fe's Canyon Road is one of the most elegant streets in New Mexico. Some of its splendid mansions belong to families who have lived in the region for generations. Others are the vacation retreats of oil tycoons from Texas. Despite such signs of wealth, 19 percent of all New Mexicans live below the poverty line. New Mexico is a state of striking contrasts. Some people are very rich; some are desperately poor; and many hover in between. How do these people earn their living? Where do they spend their money? The answers to these questions tell a great deal about New Mexico's economy.

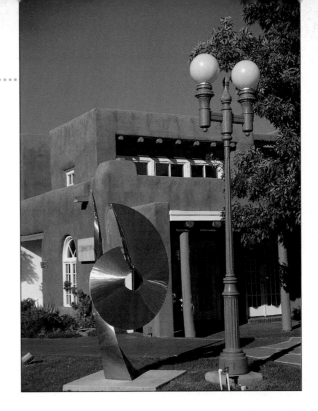

Canyon Road is one of New Mexico's wealthiest areas.

Farming, Mining, and Making Things

The gross state product (GSP) is the total value of goods and services produced in a given state. Services are jobs done for other people. Goods are products that can be sold within and outside the state. These goods can be produced through farming, mining, or manufacturing.

About 3 percent of New Mexico's GSP comes from agriculture. Beef cattle graze on the state's eastern plains. Dairy herds browse in fields along the Rio Grande. Sheep ranching is also important, especially among the Navajo and in many old Hispanic communities. Hay and alfalfa, used as livestock feed, are leading crops. Other crops include corn, wheat, sorghum, and pecans. New Mexico is the nation's foremost producer of chile peppers.

Opposite: Peppers are among New Mexico's sources of revenue.

Between 1870 and 1881, John Simpson Chisum (1824–1884) was the richest cattle rancher in the world. Chisum's ranch sprawled over 200 square miles (518 sq km) south of Fort Sum-

Money on the Hoof

ner in eastern New Mexico. More than 100,000 steers wore Chisum's famous Long Rail Brand.

Chisum began his career as a county clerk in Paris, Texas. Many Texans were growing rich in the cattle business, and Chisum was determined to follow their example. He soon found superb grazing land along New Mexico's Pecos River. Nearby Fort Sumner provided an eager market for Chisum's beef.

For more than a decade, Chisum was the sole rancher in the region. He made it clear that settlers were not welcome in his territory. But by 1881, his power began to crumble. Rustlers, or cattle thieves, made off with many of his animals. More of his herd was destroyed in warfare between the Anglos and the Apache. Other ranchers moved into the area, and Chisum's vast empire was no more. ∎

Mining accounts for 9 percent of New Mexico's GSP. Two-thirds of the state's mining income stems from petroleum and natural gas. Oil rigs tower over the plains around Artesia in the southeastern corner of the state. The smell of oil hangs in the air. Natural gas is piped from some 4,200 wells in the same region. Coal is mined in San Juan County in the mesa region of the northwest. New Mexico ranks third among the states in the production of copper.

The Tularosa Basin has rich deposits of gypsum, a chalky mineral used in making plaster and cement. The state ranks sixth in the nation in the production of molybdenum, vital in the manufacture of steel. In the production of potash, New Mexico is

Some Like It Hot!

Chile peppers come in red or green. They may be mild, zesty, or fiery hot. New Mexican farmers grow chiles of every shape, size, and variety. They are sold fresh, dried, canned, or powdered.

Chile of one kind or another is an ingredient in most traditional New Mexican dishes. It adds a bite to garden salads and puts a delicious sting into baked chicken or pork. Often chile is served to the side of the main dish, and you can add as much or as little as you choose.

New Mexicans debate the merits of one variety of chile over another. But one thing they all agree on—the spelling of their favorite spice. In the rest of the world people eat "chili," but they grow and eat "chile" in New Mexico. ■

What New Mexico Grows, Manufactures, and Mines

Agriculture	Manufacturing	Mining
Beef cattle	Electrical equipment	Natural gas
Milk	Scientific instruments	Petroleum
Hay	Food products	Copper
	Printed materials	Coal

number one in the United States. Potash is found underground in deposits of a mineral called sylvite. Most potash is used in making fertilizer.

New Mexico's towns and small cities have relatively few factories. Only 13 percent of the state's GSP comes from manufacturing. Plants in Albuquerque turn out computer chips and military communications systems. Other factories produce appliances, telephone equipment, and scientific instruments. Large oil refineries operate near Artesia and Gallup.

Belowground inside a potash mine

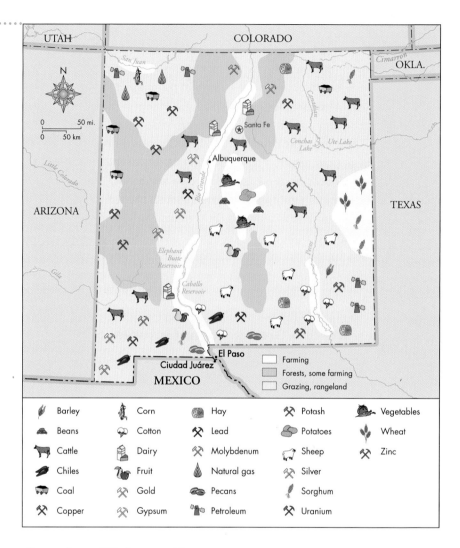

UTAH COLORADO OKLA.

ARIZONA TEXAS

MEXICO

Santa Fe
Albuquerque
El Paso
Ciudad Juárez

Farming
Forests, some farming
Grazing, rangeland

0   50 mi.
0   50 km

Barley	Corn	Hay	Potash	Vegetables	
Beans	Cotton	Lead	Potatoes	Wheat	
Cattle	Dairy	Molybdenum	Sheep	Zinc	
Chiles	Fruit	Natural gas	Silver		
Coal	Gold	Pecans	Sorghum		
Copper	Gypsum	Petroleum	Uranium		

New Mexico's natural resources

Getting Things Done

About 71 percent of the GSP in New Mexico comes from services performed within the state. Services include sales, banking, health care, and teaching. Office workers perform services, as do beauticians and taxi drivers. The private, or business, sector employs more people than any other part of New Mexico's economy. Private-sector employees work in real estate, retail sales, and many small businesses.

One of the most important industries in New Mexico is tourism. Every year about 15 million visitors pass through the state. They go skiing or bathe in the hot springs. They explore parklands and wander through art galleries. Tourists spend some $3 billion a year in New Mexico. The tourist industry creates 50,000 jobs in restaurants, hotels, shops, and resorts. Unfortunately, most of these jobs pay relatively little.

Many tourists enjoy New Mexico's state parks.

Though the majority of New Mexicans work in the private sector, the government is the state's single biggest employer. The federal government pays people to manage national forests and monuments. It employs thousands of scientists and other workers in research laboratories. About 10 percent of all New Mexicans work for the military. Kirtland and Hollaman Air Force Bases are major installations in the state.

Homes Away from Home

In 1939, Conrad Hilton (1887–1979) opened a modern ten-story hotel in Albuquerque. It was part of a growing chain of hotels that Hilton had begun building in 1918. A native of San Antonio, New Mexico, Hilton built his first hotels in New Mexico and Texas. Later he expanded to locations in California, Chicago, and New York. His hotels were known for high standards of quality. After World War II, Hilton began to open hotels overseas. At his death, Hilton Hotels stood in thirty-seven countries. ◼

Crossing the Bridge

About 10,000 people work at Los Alamos National Laboratory northwest of Santa Fe. The laboratory is a vast complex of a thousand buildings covering 43 square miles (111 sq km). Largely funded by the U.S. Department of Energy (DOE), Los Alamos is one of New Mexico's major employers.

From 1943 until 1957, Los Alamos National Laboratory was surrounded by chain-link fences and locked gates. The research carried on within its walls was considered highly sensitive for national security. Today, most of the fences are gone, and the gates stand open. To enter the lab, you simply cross the bridge over Los Alamos Canyon.

During World War II, the laboratory was a secret community where scientists developed the world's first atomic bomb. For the next fifty years, the lab supplied the nation's nuclear arsenal. After 1992, however, international tensions lessened, and the focus shifted at Los Alamos. Now its scientists are no longer building weapons. Instead, they seek ways to diffuse the weapons we have, rendering them harmless to the world. Los Alamos National Laboratory has crossed the bridge from war to peace. ■

Making Connections

Three hundred years ago only the Camino Real connected New Mexico with the rest of the world. Today, high-speed transportation and telecommunications systems link New Mexicans with every spot on the globe. U.S. Highway 85 follows the route of the old Santa Fe Trail. Altogether New Mexico has 61,000 miles

(98,170 km) of roads and highways. Railroad trains provide Albuquerque with both freight and passenger service. Ironically, the Santa Fe Railroad does not stop in Santa Fe.

Albuquerque International Airport is the biggest and busiest airport in New Mexico. It receives about 3 million passengers a year. In addition, New Mexico has 148 smaller airports.

New Mexico began publishing its first newspaper in 1834. Printed in Spanish in Santa Fe, it was called *El Crepúsculo de la Libertad*, or the *Liberty Evening News*. The *Santa Fe Republic*, the first English-language paper, went to press in 1847. Today, New Mexico has fifty newspapers, fifteen of them published daily. The *Albuquerque Journal* has the highest circulation in the state.

KOB, New Mexico's first radio station, went on the air in Albuquerque in 1922. KOB-TV began broadcasting in 1948. New Mexico now has 150 radio stations, 20 TV stations, and 6 cable TV stations. Several TV and radio stations offer programming in Spanish, as well as in Navajo and other Native American languages spoken within the state.

There are 61,000 miles of roads and railroads in New Mexico.

CHAPTER NINE

The Braid of Three Strands

New Mexico's Native Americans often speak English as well as their tribal languages.

n the words of New Mexico writer Nash Candelaria: "I am a true child of New Mexico's cultures: the Spanish whose surname I bear; the Native American which many in my family will not admit to and whose looks and complexion I share; and a dollop of Anglo like a latter day grace note to remind me that I am part of the mainstream, no matter what anyone else may surmise from my physical appearance."

Hispanics, Anglos, and Native Americans

English is the dominant language in New Mexico. But many other languages are spoken here as well. The Native Americans who live on tribal lands learn English in school. At home, however, they often prefer their native tongues. Nearly a dozen distinct American Indian languages are alive in New Mexico. They include Navajo, several Apache dialects, and a number of Pueblo languages. The Pueblo fall into four major language groups: Keresan, Tewa, Tiwa, and Towa. Though the names are confusingly similar, these are thoroughly different languages. In fact, even people from two Keresan- or Tewa-speaking pueblos may have trouble understanding one another.

Spanish is widely spoken in New Mexico. Descendants of the early Spanish colonists speak a form of the language that is unknown anywhere else in the world. It closely resembles the

Opposite: A Native American woman in Albuquerque

New Mexican Anglos speak with a variety of accents.

Some Hispanics work on ranches shearing sheep.

Habla Español?

Whether they are Anglo, Hispanic, or Native American, New Mexicans use many Spanish words in their everyday speech. Among them are *arroyo* (ah-RRO-yo), a small stream; *acequia* (ah-SEH-kee-ah), an irrigation ditch; *mesa* (MEH-sah), a steep, flat-topped hill—the word literally means "table"; *viga* (VEE-gah), a heavy wooden beam or rafter; and *fiesta* (fee-ES-tah), festival or party. ▪

Spanish that was spoken in Spain four hundred years ago. Newcomers from Mexico also speak Spanish, the modern variety. They sometimes complain that they cannot understand long-established New Mexicans.

Even Anglo New Mexicans speak with an assortment of accents. Migrants from Texas have a telltale drawl. Those who hail from the northern states have clipped Yankee speech. It is almost impossible to decide how a "typical New Mexican" should sound.

According to census figures, 9 percent of all New Mexicans are Native Americans. New Mexico has two Apache reservations and nineteen pueblos. About one-third of the great Navajo reservation is in New Mexico, with the rest in Arizona. In all, more than 10 percent of New Mexico's land is in the hands of American Indian nations.

Hispanics make up 42 percent of New Mexico's population. This figure includes both old-line families and recent immigrants from Latin America. Many Spanish families live on land that has been handed down since

Navajo Fry Bread

Ingredients:

    vegetable oil
    3 cups flour
    2 tablespoons baking powder
    1 teaspoon salt
    1 tablespoon shortening
    1 cup warm water
    cornmeal

Directions:

Put 2 to 3 inches of oil into a deep skillet and heat until the oil starts to pop.

Meanwhile, combine flour, baking powder, and salt. Cut in 1 tablespoon of shortening. Slowly add water or milk. Form the dough into several balls (the size is up to you). Powder a surface and a rolling pin with cornmeal, and roll out the balls of dough until they are 1/4-inch thick.

With help from your mom or dad, fry the dough one at a time, turning when it becomes golden—about 1 to 2 minutes for each side.

Drain fry bread on paper towels, and serve hot.

Navajo fry bread can be served plain or with powdered sugar, honey, cinnamon, or salsa.

colonial times. New arrivals from Mexico tend to live in Albuquerque and other cities, where jobs are most plentiful. Some find work on farms and ranches, picking fruit, shearing sheep, and herding cattle.

About 66 percent of New Mexicans are Anglos. The term *Anglo* loosely describes anyone of European heritage who does not have a Spanish surname. Anglos are relative newcomers to New Mexico. They began migrating west from Texas early in the

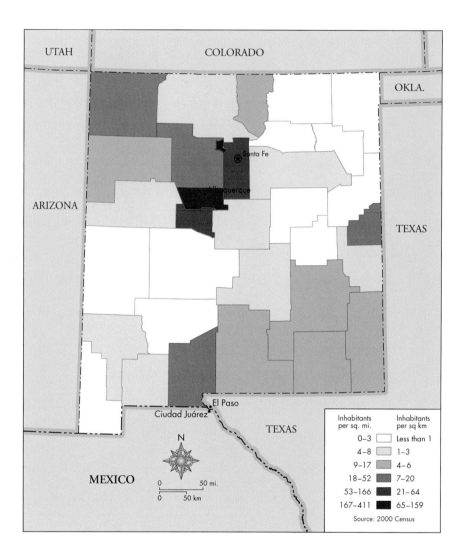

New Mexico's population density

Inhabitants per sq. mi.		Inhabitants per sq km	
0–3	☐	Less than 1	
4–8		1–3	
9–17		4–6	
18–52		7–20	
53–166		21–64	
167–411	■	65–159	

Source: 2000 Census

nineteenth century. In the twentieth century, Anglo migration became a flood as New Mexico was "discovered" by the rest of the country.

New Mexico's three cultures—Hispanic, Anglo, and Native American—are woven together like a braid with three strands. Many New Mexicans, like the writer Nash Candelaria, carry traces

of all three. New Mexico also has small numbers of African-Americans and Asians. The more the state grows, the more diverse its population becomes.

Today, New Mexico is one of the nation's most thinly populated states. Though it is the fifth largest in area, it had only 1,819,046 people in 2000. On average, the state has 15 people per square mile (5.8 per sq km). In contrast, tiny New Jersey has 1,134 people for every square mile (438 per sq km) of soil.

Population figures can be misleading, however. Though some New Mexicans live in wide-open spaces, about one-third of them are crammed into Albuquerque and its suburbs. The majority—73 percent—of all New Mexicans are classified as urban dwellers. To demographers, or population experts, this means that they live in towns of 2,500 people or more. Las Cruces is the second-largest city, followed by Santa Fe, the state capital. Other leading cities include Roswell, Rio Rancho, and Farmington.

Population of New Mexico's Major Cities (2000)

Albuquerque	448,607
Las Cruces	74,267
Santa Fe	62,203
Rio Rancho	51,765
Roswell	45,293
Farmington	37,844

The University of New Mexico is the state's leading college.

Going to School

Most children in Albuquerque and other cities attend neighborhood schools. In remote parts of the state, buses collect children from ranches and villages, carrying them to schools that may be 20 or 30 miles (32 to 40 km) from home. Most pueblos and reservations have their own school programs.

The first schools in New Mexico were run by Catholic friars during the Spanish colonial era. Public schools began to serve New Mexico's children in 1891. Today, state law requires all New Mexican children to attend school between the ages of five and sixteen. In 1995, there were 303,792 pupils enrolled in public elementary and secondary schools.

About 71 percent of New Mexico's students graduate from high school. Many of them go on to earn college and graduate degrees. The University of New Mexico at Albuquerque is the state's leading institution of higher learning. Other colleges and universities include New Mexico State University at Las Cruces,

To Begin at the Beginning

Within every religious tradition, people tell stories to explain the creation of the world as we know it. Such tales are referred to as creation myths. The Pueblo people of New Mexico have several variations on this creation story.

Long, long ago, a stream flowed deep underground. Living matter in its waters shaped itself into insects, lizards, birds, and animals. Finally, it formed human beings. One day, these people grew tired of the dark place where they lived. They climbed until at last they reached a lake. Joyfully, they burst the surface into sunlight. The people clambered onto dry land, followed by all the other creatures. These were the ancestors of the Pueblo people who live in New Mexico today. ■

Eastern New Mexico University in Portales, New Mexico Highlands University in Las Vegas, St. John's College in Santa Fe, College of the Southwest in Hobbs, and Western New Mexico University in Silver City.

The Life of the Spirit

Christian ideas and practices weave through the lives of New Mexico's Native Americans. But most native people still hold traditional beliefs as well. American Indian parents tell their children ancient myths that they learned from their own parents. On Roman Catholic feast days, the Pueblo celebrate with both Christian prayers and tribal chants and dances.

About one-third of all New Mexicans are members of the Roman Catholic Church. Catholic churches stand in nearly every town and village in the state. The archbishop of the Southwestern Diocese sits at the St. Francis Cathedral in Santa Fe. Built in 1869 by Archbishop Jean-Baptiste Lamy, the cathedral is the most famous church in the state.

A Man of the People

In 1851, the Reverend Jean-Baptiste Lamy (1814–1888) arrived in Santa Fe to serve as its Roman Catholic bishop. Lamy soon won the love of New Mexico's people. One acquaintance later wrote, "[He was] equally at home in the hut of the Indian, the cabin of the miner, or in the Vatican at the feet of the Pontiff."

Lamy directed the building of the St. Francis Cathedral, which went into construction in 1869. He was elevated to the rank of archbishop and served in that position until his death. He was deeply mourned by the people he had served and is still remembered as a man who put Christian ideals into practice. ■

Suffering with Christ

During the nineteenth century, a group of passionately devout Roman Catholics arose in northern New Mexico. Known as the *Penitentes,* or Repentant Ones, they tried to experience the sufferings Jesus Christ endured on Earth. Sometimes they whipped themselves until they fell unconscious. Every Easter, one member of the group was tied to a heavy wooden cross.

The Penitentes have abandoned such practices, but they are still a presence in New Mexico. Known as the Brotherhood of Light, they help the sick and the poor. ■

Baptist missionaries reached New Mexico in 1849. They were soon followed by Mormons from Utah. Today, New Mexico has numerous Protestant denominations, including Baptists, Methodists, Presbyterians, and Episcopalians. About 6,000 Jews live in the state, chiefly in Albuquerque and Santa Fe. A small Hindu community thrives in Santa Cruz, and a Muslim mosque was built in the Chama Valley in 1980.

The San Miguel Chapel in Santa Fe

CHAPTER TEN

Rich Harvest from a Dry Land

Painter Georgia O'Keeffe described her first summer in New Mexico in 1930 as follows: "The first summer I spent in New Mexico I was a little surprised because there were so few flowers. There was no rain so the flowers didn't come. Bones were easy to find, so I began collecting bones. . . . I had to go home. What could I take with me of my country to keep me working on it? I had collected many bones and finally decided the best thing I could do was to take with me a barrel of bones, so I took a barrel of bones."

Red and black designs are common in Isleta pottery.

A Leaning toward the Arts

When Georgia O'Keeffe visited New Mexico in 1930, she was dazzled by the stark beauty of the mountains and deserts. Sometimes she feared she could not do the land justice in her paintings. She spent the next fifty years trying to capture its essence on canvas.

Georgia O'Keeffe is the most famous New Mexico painter of modern times. But New Mexico has inspired artists for untold centuries. Hundreds of years ago, Native Americans made dyes from wild plants and berries. They used these colors to adorn their clay pots and bowls. Over time, different Indian groups developed distinctive decorative patterns. These unique pottery styles are very much alive today. Potters at Isleta Pueblo make red and black

Opposite: A buffalo skull in the New Mexican sand

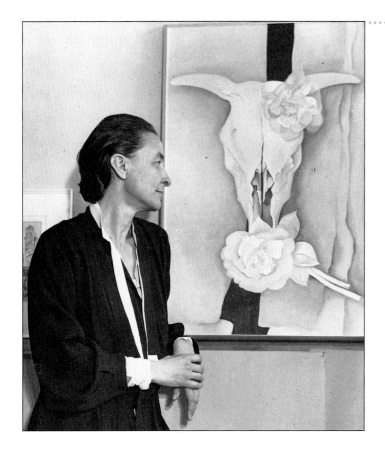

Flowers and Bones

Georgia O'Keeffe (1887–1986) grew up on a farm in Wisconsin. She studied painting in Chicago and New York City. During the 1920s, her haunting, abstract paintings won widespread acclaim. The country around Taos, New Mexico, provided O'Keeffe with lasting inspiration. She often painted large pictures of flowers or of animal bones, such as those she found in the New Mexican desert.

In 1959, O'Keeffe took her first trip in an airplane. She was intrigued by the aerial view of the earth. During the 1960s, many of her canvases depicted the earth and clouds as seen from high above. ■

geometric designs on a white background. The pottery of Zia Pueblo often bears the familiar sun sign. Many Native American potters have won national and international acclaim. Their work fetches lofty prices in the galleries of Taos and Santa Fe.

New Mexico's art scene is among its foremost attractions. Painters, sculptors, and potters come to study and to work. Often they use Spanish and Indian motifs in new ways, turning age-old patterns into work that is modern and fresh.

Native Americans were the first architects in New Mexico. Visitors still marvel at the brilliant design of Pueblo Bonito and other Anasazi creations. Hispanic and Anglo New Mexicans

Living Traditions

As a girl growing up at San Ildefonso Pueblo, Maria Martinez (1885?–1980) learned from her aunt to make pottery. She gathered clay near her home, shaped it into pots, and fired them in a pit to make them strong. After she married, Martinez continued to make her pots and jars, which her husband, Julian, painted with traditional designs.

In 1908, a team of archaeologists began to excavate an Anasazi village near San Ildefonso. One of the scientists showed Martinez examples of black Anasazi pottery painted with dark designs. After some experimenting, Martinez and her husband produced pots like those found in the ruined village. The pots had a glossy black sheen, and the designs were made in a duller black. Maria Martinez began to sell her black-on-black pottery in shops in Santa Fe. She taught the technique to other women and men at the pueblo.

Martinez's work won her national recognition. She was awarded honorary doctorate degrees from three universities. She and her husband demonstrated their pottery-making at world's fairs in San Diego and St. Louis. In 1934, Maria Martinez was invited to a reception at the White House. The first lady, Eleanor Roosevelt, gave a moving speech. She said that Native American art is a priceless part of our national heritage. She praised Maria Martinez for helping to keep that art alive for future generations. ■

The adobe style is still popular in New Mexican buildings

borrowed the use of adobe brick as they built their homes and churches. Though true adobe is seldom used today, many new buildings still strive for the adobe look. The low, flat-roofed buildings in earth-colored shades fit perfectly into the southwestern landscape.

Legacy of the Anasazi

Ruins of ancient Anasazi architecture are preserved at Chaco Culture National Historic Park near Farmington, New Mexico. The finest of the park's offerings is Pueblo Bonito (Pretty Town), a stone and adobe "apartment house" built onto a cliffside. Originally, Pueblo Bonito contained more than 800 rooms and kivas. ■

Taking the Big Picture

As a young man growing up in California, Ansel Adams (1902–1984) was devoted to the piano. He also loved to take pictures. In 1927, Adams published a book of photographs he had taken in the California mountains. Its success prompted him to make photography his new career.

Ansel Adams helped raise photography to a form of art. He encouraged young photographers to exhibit their work and helped create photography programs at several universities.

Adams made many trips to New Mexico. In 1941, he took one of his most famous photos. *Moonrise: Hernandez, New Mexico* is a magnificent twilight landscape of craggy mountains.

In 1936, Adams was appointed director of the Sierra Club, a leading conservation organization. Through his photos, Adams made a plea for the preservation of our last wild places. ■

Words and Music

Many writers have been entranced by New Mexico. The state was an inspiration for Willa Cather (1873–1947). Her novel *Death Comes for the Archbishop* was inspired by the story of Archbishop Lamy of Santa Fe.

Many New Mexico writers explore the unique blending of cultures that occurs in the state. Tony Hillerman of Albuquerque (1925–) writes a series of detective novels featuring Navajo police officers Joe Leaphorn and Jim Chee. The books deal with the collision of Navajo and non-Indian cultures. Leslie M. Silko (1948–) is a writer of mixed Anglo, Hispanic, and Pueblo

Tony Hillerman

The Coal Miner's Son

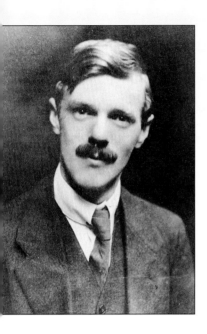

David Herbert (D. H.) Lawrence (1885–1930) was the son of an English coal miner. He defied his working-class origins by attending Oxford University. With works such as *The Rainbow* (1915), *Women in Love* (1916), and *Lady Chatterley's Lover* (1928), Lawrence became one of the leading English novelists of the twentieth century.

Lawrence's work often deals with the evils of industrial society. He found a very different way of life when he visited New Mexico in 1922. Yet even there, amid the wild mountains, he sensed change and loss.

On a hike in the Lobo Canyon of the Sangre de Cristo Mountains, Lawrence once saw two men carrying a cougar they had killed. In a poem called "Mountain Lion," Lawrence wrote sadly about the death of the large cat.

Between 1922 and 1925, D. H. Lawrence spent most of his time on a ranch near Taos. Every year, dedicated fans of his novels visit the D. H. Lawrence Ranch and pay their respects at the site where his ashes are buried. ▪

descent. She grew up in the Laguna Pueblo community, the setting for her 1974 novel, *Ceremony*. John Nichols wrote about the conflicts between Hispanics and Anglos in *The Milagro Beanfield War* (1974).

The *corridos* of New Mexico's Hispanic people are a form of musical poetry. These ballads are sung in Spanish to lilting guitars. They tell of love, betrayal, and the homesickness of those who have crossed the border from Mexico.

New Mexicans love music of every variety. Traditional chants accompanied by drums and rattles are part of most Native American ceremonies. Many Anglos favor country and western music.

The Cradle of Rock 'n' Roll

In the 1950s, Norman Petty opened a small recording studio in Clovis, New Mexico. One of Petty's first clients was a young musician named Charles Hardin "Buddy" Holly (1937–1959). Born in Lubbock, Texas, Holly was a pioneer in the new music called rock 'n' roll. He was a guitarist and composer who combined elements of country music with lively rock rhythms. Holly recorded some of his most famous songs in Clovis, including "Peggy Sue" and "That'll Be the Day."

Tragically, Buddy Holly died in a plane crash when he was only twenty-two years old. Each year, rock 'n' roll fans pour into New Mexico for the annual Clovis Music Festival. As a highlight of the festival, Buddy Holly's widow opens the old recording studio to the public. ■

Classical music lovers flock to Santa Fe every summer to enjoy the world-renowned Santa Fe Opera. Opera tickets are usually sold out a year in advance.

Fun and Festivals

New Mexico has no major-league sports teams. Many New Mexicans root for such nearby pro teams as the Dallas Cowboys or the Denver Broncos. During football season the Lobos of the University of New Mexico draw cheering crowds to their stadium in

Albuquerque. In 1970, New Mexico State University's basketball team finished third in the NCAA tournament.

Though they have no pro teams, New Mexicans love to watch and take part in athletics of all kinds. At rodeos, daring (or foolhardy) young riders test their skill with wildly bucking horses. Sunland Park near Las Cruces hosts horse races throughout the winter. In the summer, racing fans go to Ruidoso Downs outside Mesa Park.

New Mexico's steep mountain slopes lure skiers from all over the world. Hiking and mountain biking are popular throughout the state. Conditions are perfect for fly-fishing on the San Juan River and at Elephant Butte Lake. New Mexico's lakes and streams hold catfish, large- and smallmouth bass, rainbow trout, and kokanee salmon. The cutthroat trout is a coveted prize.

Not everyone in New Mexico gets excited about sports. But nearly everybody loves a festival, or fiesta. Fiestas honor saints, heroes, or special events in history. They are celebrated with food, music, processions, and good fellowship.

The town of Chimayo carries on a thousand-year-old Spanish tradition with its Fiesta de Santiago. An all-night pageant recalls the Spanish hero Santiago, who fought off Moorish invaders in the ninth century A.D. In Bernalillo, the Fiesta de San Lorenzo is held every August. Beautifully dressed dancers depict the story of Spain's conquest of Mexico in 1519. Now and then, the show is interrupted by a noisy troop of clowns called the *abuelos* (pronounced ah-BWEH-los), or grandparents. The abuelos threaten to whip any children who fidget during the performance.

One of the biggest festivals in all New Mexico is the Fiesta de

Ride 'Em, Cowboy!

The smell of horses! The roaring of bulls! The cheers and applause of a crowd! This is the excitement of a rodeo. As in any sport, rodeo contestants are expected to play by the rules. In bareback riding, a cowboy must remain on a bronco's back for eight seconds, spurring his mount the entire time. In barrel racing, a women's sport, a cowgirl must ride her horse in and out among three barrels without knocking them over.

Rodeos evolved in the late nineteenth century as entertainment when cowhands gathered after long cattle drives. During the 1930s, the first organized rodeos were held for paying spectators. Today, some "all-girl" rodeos exclusively feature women's events, including goat roping and calf roping. In one women's event, known as steer undecorating, a woman on horseback must capture a ribbon that is taped to the back of a running steer. Animal protection agencies monitor rodeos to ensure that animals are not mistreated. ■

Up, Up, and Away!

Hot-air balloon enthusiasts flock to New Mexico each October for the Albuquerque International Balloon Festival. Begun in 1972, the festival is the biggest gathering of balloonists in the United States. During ten fun-filled days, some 500 balloons lift off and sail above the city, setting the sky ablaze with color! ■

New Mexicans enjoy markets, fairs, and festivals throughout the year.

Santa Fe, held each September. Pueblo craftspeople, scientists from Los Alamos, painters, tourists, ranch hands, and miners pour into the city. The streets overflow with people speaking English, Spanish, and several Native American languages. On the first evening, the excited crowd packs Fort Marcy Park and watches the giant figure of Zozobra go up in flames. Another year has ended. A new year is about to begin.

Timeline

United States History

The first permanent British **1607**
settlement is established in North
America at Jamestown.

Pilgrims found Plymouth Colony, the **1620**
second permanent British settlement.

America declares its independence **1776**
from England.

Treaty of Paris officially ends the **1783**
Revolutionary War in America.

U.S. Constitution is written. **1787**

Louisiana Purchase almost doubles **1803**
the size of the United States.

U.S. and Britain **1812-15**
fight the War of 1812.

New Mexico State History

1539   Father Marcos de Niza searches for
the Seven Cities of Gold.

1610   Pedro de Peralta establishes Santa Fe
as the capital of New Mexico.

1680   The Pueblo people revolt against
Spanish rule.

1692-96   The Spanish retake control of
New Mexico.

1706   Francisco Cuervo y Valdes establishes
Albuquerque.

1821   Mexico (including the territory of
New Mexico) gains independence
from Spain.

1846   General Stephen W. Kearny
announces U.S. control over New
Mexico.

1848   The Treaty of Guadalupe Hidalgo
cedes New Mexico to the United
States.

1850   The Territory of New Mexico is
established.

United States History

The North and South fight **1861–65** each other in the American Civil War.

The United States is **1917–18** involved in World War I.

The stock market crashes, plunging **1929** the United States into the Great Depression.

The United States fights in **1941–45** World War II.

The United States becomes a **1945** charter member of the United Nations.

The United States fights **1951–53** in the Korean War.

The U.S. Congress enacts a series of **1964** groundbreaking civil rights laws.

The United States **1964–73** engages in the Vietnam War.

The United States and other **1991** nations fight the brief Persian Gulf War against Iraq.

New Mexico State History

1880 Sheriff Pat Garrett kills Billy the Kid.

1912 New Mexico becomes the forty-seventh state.

1916 Mexican general Pancho Villa kills sixteen people in Columbus, New Mexico.

1922 Oil is discovered in San Juan County.

1943 Hundreds of scientists begin working secretly on the atomic bomb at Los Alamos.

1948 New Mexico's Native Americans gain the right to vote.

1992 Los Alamos National Laboratory begins seeking ways to diffuse nuclear weapons.

Fast Facts

Roadrunner

Yucca flower

Statehood date	January 6, 1912, the 47th state
Origin of state name	The Spaniards in Mexico applied the term "New Mexico" to the area north and west of the Rio Grande during the sixteenth century.
State capital	Santa Fe
State nickname	The Land of Enchantment
State motto	*Crescit Eundo* ("It grows as it goes")
State bird	Roadrunner
State flower	Yucca flower
State animal	Black bear
State fish	Cutthroat trout
State gem	Turquoise
State songs	"*Así Es Nuevo Méjico*" and "O Fair New Mexico"
State tree	Piñon pine
State fair	Albuquerque (mid-September)
Total area; rank	121,598 sq. mi. (314,937 sq km); 5th
Land; rank	121,364 sq. mi. (314,331 sq km); 5th
Water; rank	234 sq. mi. (606 sq km); 47th

Albuquerque

Inland water; **rank**	234 sq. mi. (606 sq km); 44th
Geographic center	Torrance, 12 miles (19 km) southwest of Willard
Latitude and longitude	New Mexico is located approximately between 31° 20′ and 37° N and 103° and 109° W
Highest point	Wheeler Peak, 13,161 feet (4,011 m)
Lowest point	Red Bluff Reservoir, 2,842 feet (866 m)
Largest city	Albuquerque
Number of counties	33
Population; rank	1,819,046 (2000 census); 36th
Density	15 persons per sq. mi. (5.8 per sq km)
Population distribution	73% urban, 27% rural

Ethnic distribution (does not equal 100%)		
White		66.8%
Hispanic		42.1%
Native American		9.5%
African-American		1.9%
Asian and Pacific Islanders		1.2%

Record high temperature	16°F (47°C) at Orogrande on July 14, 1934, and at Artesia on June 29, 1918
Record low temperature	−50°F (−46°C) at Gavilan, near Lindrith, on February 1, 1951
Average July temperature	74°F (23°C)
Average January temperature	34°F (1°C)

A Native American woman

Carlsbad Caverns

| Average January temperature | 34°F (1°C) |
| Average annual precipitation | 13 inches (33 cm) |

Natural Areas and Historic Sites

National Parks

Carlsbad Caverns National Park is a series of connected caverns and has one of the world's largest underground spaces.

National Monuments

Aztec Ruins National Monument preserves the ruins of an ancient Pueblo people in the Animas River valley.

Bandelier National Monument contains the ruins of ancient Pueblo peoples.

Capulin Volcano National Monument features a 1,000 foot (300-m) extinct volcano cinder cone.

El Malpais National Monument is rich in Pueblo history and features a 17-mile (27-km)-long lava tube system as well as ice caves.

El Morro National Monument is a sandstone cliff, more popularly known as Inscription Rock.

Fort Union National Monument contains the adobe ruins of Fort Union, the last of three forts active in New Mexico between 1851 and 1891.

Gila Cliff Dwellings National Monument preserves cliff dwellings constructed by the Mogollon.

Cliff dwellings

New Mexican desert

Petroglyph National Monument preserves ancient pictures drawn on lava.

Salinas Pueblo National Monument contains the ruins of historic Pueblo villages at Gran Quivira, Abó, and Quarai in the Salinas Valley.

White Sands National Monument contains the largest gypsum dune field in the world.

National Historical Parks

Chaco Culture National Historical Park preserves 13 major ruins and more than 300 smaller sites that are among the finest ancient structures in the United States.

Pecos National Historical Park contains the ruins of two Spanish missions from the fifteenth century.

Gila National Forest

Sports Teams

NCAA Teams (Division I)

New Mexico University State University Aggies

University of New Mexico Lobos

Cultural Institutions

Libraries

Albuquerque Public Library is the largest public library in the state.

The Thomas Branigan Memorial Library (Las Cruces)

Museums

Museum of New Mexico (Santa Fe) located in the Palace of the Governors includes the Museum of Fine Arts, the Museum of Indian Arts and Culture, and the Museum of International Folk Art.

The Wheelwright Museum of the American Indian (Santa Fe)

The Georgia O'Keeffe Museum (Santa Fe)

The Albuquerque Museum has a fine collection of European and Indian art.

Performing Arts

New Mexico has two major opera companies, one major symphony orchestra, and one major dance company.

Universities and Colleges

In the mid-1990s, New Mexico had twenty-three public and nine private institutions of higher learning.

Georgia O'Keeffe

Zia sun hot-air balloon

Pottery from Santa Fe

Annual Events

January–March

King's Day Dances in most of the Indian pueblos (January 6)

Winter Festival in Red River (January)

Bach Festival in Santa Fe (early February)

Great Overland Windsail Race in Lordsburg (March)

Dances at most Indian pueblos (Easter).

April–June

Green Corn Dance at San Felipe Pueblo (May 1)

Ralph Edwards Festival in Truth or Consequences (early May)

Four-Corners Hot-Air Balloon Fiesta near Farmington (late May)

Taos Spring Arts Celebration (May–June)

New Mexico Arts and Crafts Fair in Albuquerque (late June).

July–September

Apache Indian Ceremonial in Mescalero (Fourth of July weekend)

Rodeo de Santa Fe (mid-July)

Puye Cliff Ceremonial at Santa Clara Pueblo (last Saturday and Sunday in July)

Green Corn Dance at Santo Domingo Pueblo (August 4)

Billy the Kid Pageant in Lincoln (early August)

Inter-Tribal Indian Ceremonial in Gallup (mid-August)

Santa Fe Indian Market (late August)

Great American Duck Race in Deming (late August)

Zozobra is set on fire

Fiesta de Santa Fe

Fiesta de Santa Fe (mid-September)

New Mexico State Fair in Albuquerque (mid-September)

Feast Day in Taos Pueblo (late September)

October–December

Eastern New Mexico State Fair in Roswell (early October)

Festival of the Arts in Santa Fe (early October)

Navajo Fair in Shiprock (early October)

Taos Festival of Arts (early October)

International Balloon Fiesta in Albuquerque (mid-October)

Shalako Dance, Zuni Pueblo (late November/early December)

Christmas Eve dances in mission churches at many Indian pueblos
(December 24)

Christmas Eve Luminaria Tours in Albuquerque (December 24)

Kit Carson

Georgia O'Keeffe

Famous People

Christopher (Kit) Carson (1809–1868)	Trapper and soldier
John Simpson Chisum (1824–1884)	Cattleman
David Herbert (D. H.) Lawrence (1885–1930)	Author
William Henry (Bill) Mauldin (1921–)	Cartoonist
William Henry (Billy the Kid) McCarty (1859–1889)	Outlaw
Georgia O'Keeffe (1887–1986)	Artist
Albert Pike (1809–1891)	Soldier
Ernest Thompson Seton (1860–1946)	Author and naturalist

To Find Out More

History

- Anderson, Joan, and George Ancona (illus.). *Cowboys: Roundup on an American Ranch*. New York: Scholastic, 1996.

- Doherty, Katherine, and Craig Doherty. *The Zunis*. Chicago: Franklin Watts, 1994.

- Early, Theresa S. *New Mexico*. Minneapolis: Lerner, 1993.

- Fradin, Dennis Brindell. *New Mexico*. Chicago: Childrens Press, 1993.

- Thompson, Kathleen. *New Mexico*. Austin, Tex.: Raintree/Steck-Vaughn, 1996.

Fiction

- Krumgold, Joseph. *And Now, Miguel*. New York: Crowell, 1953.

- Meyer, Carolyn. *Rio Grande Stories*. New York: Gulliver Books, 1994.

Biographies

- Morris, Juddi. *Tending the Fire: The Story of Maria Martinez*. Flagstaff, Ariz.: Rising Moon, 1997.

- O'Connor, Barbara. *The Soldier's Voice: The Story of Ernie Pyle*. Minneapolis: Carolrhoda Books, 1996.

- Sanford, William R. *Kit Carson: Frontier Scout*. Springfield, N.J.: Enslow, 1996.

Websites

■ **New Mexico Department of Tourism**
http://www.newmexico.org
A wide-ranging introduction to the many wonders of New Mexico

■ **State of New Mexico Government Information Web**
http://www.state.nm.us
The official state website of New Mexico

Addresses

■ **Department of Tourism**
Lamy Building
491 Old Santa Fe Trail
Santa Fe, NM 87503
For information on the tourism and history of New Mexico

■ **Legislative Council Service**
334 State Capitol
Santa Fe, NM 87503
For information on New Mexico's government

Index

Page numbers in *italics* indicate illustrations.

Meet the Author

I'm Deborah Kent. I grew up in Little Falls, New Jersey, where I was the first blind student to attend the local public school. I received my B.A. in English from Oberlin College and a master's degree from Smith College School for Social Work. For four years, I worked at the University Settlement House in New York City. Then I decided to pursue my lifelong dream to become a writer. I moved to San Miguel de Allende in Mexico, a town with an active colony of writers and artists. There I wrote my first young-adult novel, *Belonging*.

I lived in Mexico for five years. Shortly after returning to the United States, I rented a house in Santa Fe, New Mexico. After my experience in Mexico, I felt very much at home in Santa Fe, with its many artists and its Spanish and Mexican atmosphere. As I worked on this book I fondly remembered hikes in the mountains and the wonderful scent of piñon pine.

Today, I work full-time as a writer of books for children and young adults. My books include novels, biographies, and many titles on history and geography. For Children's Press I have written books in the Cities of the World series as well as the America the Beautiful series. I live in Chicago with my husband, children's-book writer R. Conrad Stein, and our daughter Janna.

Photo Credits